Behind The Looking Glass

A Journey Of Self-Renewal

Razy Hague

ISBN: 978-1-95-163079-9

To my children

Thank you!

You walk with me on this journey in every step of my struggles, if it wasn't for your unwavering support, I wouldn't recover as well. Thank you for being the source of comfort in my life. I love you with all my heart and all of my being.

Acknowledgment

With the deep gratitude to those who help me on this journey:

To my family, thank you for being there for me and patiently waiting so that I could finish this book. I feel so fortunate to have each one of you in my life.

To my dear friends, thank you for your everlasting friendship, your alliances were so valued and cherished.

I owe a special thanks to my dear friend, Ann. I am indebted for your editorial advice and helpful suggestions.

To my colleagues, thank you for not giving up on me, and kindly covering for my classes as I was in recovery.

"Health is the greatest gift, contentment the greatest wealth, faithfulness the best relationship."
-Buddha

"Every good relationship, especially marriage, is based on respect. If it's not based on respect, nothing that appears to be good will last very long."
-Amy Grant

"Freedom means you are unobstructed in living your life as you choose. Anything less is a form of slavery."
-Wayne Dyer

"What you get by achieving your goals is not as important as what you become by achieving your goals."
-Henry David Thoreau

"A wise woman wishes to be no one's enemy; a wise woman refuses to be anyone's victim."
-Maya Angelou

Preface

My childhood molded me to be an optimist, but life's experiences gave me the wisdom to be more realistic. This book invites you into my professional and personal life experiences. I was born and raised in Iran, but have lived in the U.S. for the past forty years. I treasure all the teaching opportunities I have had, and I was looking forward to the many more years of teaching and career progress. However, I encountered unexpected obstacles which changed my path.

Those obstacles began with my marriage to a husband who transformed from being my biggest champion to someone who pressured me into abandoning my plans for career advancement. I abandoned those hopes because of promises he made but didn't keep. After teaching for thirteen years at a local college, I had a serious car accident that robbed me of my health and financial independence. My sense of identity was shaken when my doctors suggested that teaching was no longer a suitable profession for me.

The darkness of uncertainty then clouded my personal life, pushing me to question my husband's sincerity about the promises he had made to me. A mysterious legal document was his method of avoiding obligations, forcing me to take legal action and file for divorce. Only then did I uncover the fact that this secret document was a forged prenuptial agreement that I had never seen before.

When I sought justice, I was faced with an eye-opening dysfunctional court system where, instead of impartiality, I found a place where one gender was denigrated over the other. Women may have gained important rights, yet that equality paled in the face of biased judges, when they take sides in gender conflicts to undermine those gains. I subsequently lost faith in the ethics of the court system and was prompted to pen this book. I chose to bring my truth into the light in order to promote reforms in our legal system. We need to advocate for social change and to ensure that our judges are a voice for human dignity.

It took a brush with death for me to truly see the state of my marriage. But a troubling car accident also was a blessing in disguise, because in the process of recovery I realized the true sources of my strength. I hope my story encourages you to seek guidance as you make important decisions in your life, especially if you are navigating a fickle court system.

Contents

Chapter 1
Shattered Reality

That morning, as I prepared myself for another day of teaching, I could never have imagined that my life would take such an unexpected turn. While I was getting ready for my work, I had done some household chores so that I could squeeze in an hour of *"me time"* at the local gym after returning home.

My husband, Alan, had retired the previous year, and since then I had been the only early riser. As I was rushing out of the bedroom, he rolled over and rose from his slumber momentarily. With half-closed eyes, he informed me about our tax filing: *"Razy, leave your W2 form out. I'm finishing up our taxes."* His voice was muffled by blankets and pillows that he habitually arranged around himself every night. He shielded his eyes from the light and went back to sleep, without even acknowledging my 'good morning.' I glanced at my watch, and with no time to look for my W2 form, I dashed out of the house.

A beautiful spring morning greeted me outside. My mood changed as I saw our front yard packed with colorful blooms of the flowers that I had planted a month ago. Witnessing their conversion into bursts of color helped me refocus my thoughts, and prepared me for another fulfilling day with my students. Even though my earnings were meager, the recognition from my students was all I needed. I valued their boldness and enjoyed their enthusiasm when their faces lit up with excitement. My incentives were those magical moments with my students.

At school, time slipped by quickly as always. Once the clock ticked past 4:00 p.m., I ran out of the classroom to have time for a grocery stop. My little break before heading home, I thought with a weary smile.

Home was no longer a quiet retreat but instead had become a noisy place after Alan's retirement. His obsession with day trading consumed every day. In the background, the television blared with CNBC snippets on stock trading. He wouldn't leave the house until the markets had closed. His evenings were devoted to drinking, sports, and crappy movies. Regardless of his flaws and mine, I remained committed. I kept trying to engage him more in our life, hoping he would listen.

As I was preparing dinner, Alan announced from the living room: *"Going out for a walk!"* The moment he left the house, I was alone with my thoughts.

For some time now, I was desperate to resolve some of our outstanding issues. My mind raced back to the many arguments we had been having. Each time, I tiptoed all around these subjects, pressing him to hear me out. Each time, he would invent a way to brush away my concerns. The discussions had grown into an emotional tug of war, both sides struggling to maintain their positions. I felt like I was a gymnast trying to compete in a soccer match, falling flat on my face.

Recently, I had updated my list of concerns, adding *"where to retire."* I had tried all sorts of approaches, but none of them had worked. The curious and sweet approach, the confident but firm approach, and the sensible and logical approach. I loathed the stagnation and feeling of helplessness in my marriage. My newest method was to be forward and blunt. It was a gamble. Still, I had to try.

At the dinner table, I looked at Alan to gauge his mood.

He was busy with his dinner. I blurted, *"So, when do you think we should move or retire?"*

"Well, we don't have to move," he said dismissively. *"There is nothing wrong with the house we live in."* He gave me a confident smile to throw off my concerns. He noticed the scowl on my face and stopped smiling.

"You assured me that we'd move someplace else for our retirement," I protested, trying to contain my frustration.

"Look, it is cheaper here," he argued tensely.

My blood began to boil. I reminded him, *"If you want to stay here, you need to add my name to the house we live in!"*

"This is your house, sweetheart," he said, ratcheting up the charm. *"And you have nothing to worry about."*

It was becoming evident that it would be more productive writing a letter to Congress than arguing with my husband. Adding my name to our home had been a point of contention since we married. He had purchased the house a year before and promised me he would add my name to the house as soon as we were married. Since then, he had clearly avoided the subject.

It seemed peculiar that in this heated moment, he chose to remind me that I had forgotten to leave my W2 forms out. Talk about a poor sense of timing.

"You want my W2s? Get them yourself!"

I grabbed my purse and made sure to slam the door loudly, but not hard enough to damage it on my way out. I was in a state of sheer aggravation, so I headed to the gym to cool off. As I drove, all sorts of negative rationalizations swirled in my mind. Alan was a confusing man. He could be such a jerk all the while seeming like a perfectly nice guy. I tried to convince myself that he would soon see the error of his ways.

Suddenly my mind switched gears. I found myself thinking about our last New Year's Eve with out-of-town guests, and our travels to my children's graduations. My memories came in reverse, taking me to my sister's wedding and then to my last conversation with my father. My mind kept traveling back to the moments when my daughter was little. I tried to comprehend the whirlwind tour of the past I was on, but I was unable to escape the mental wormhole. Instead, I lingered with my most precious thoughts, singing songs to my newborn son and playing with his tiny hands. I wondered, 'Am I dead,' as I woke up to thick darkness with the most severe pain imaginable.

I opened my eyes and knew I was trapped inside the car. I could not move at all, though I tried. Helpless, I began to gag on the smoke and soot that surrounded me. I thought of my children, grateful they weren't with me to suffer in this moment of agony. It took me a while to notice what was left of the inside of the car. I could see the twisted metal and a mangled dashboard. As the smoke lifted, I saw faces peering in from the dark outside; the images were blurry, but it was clear that everyone was staring at me.

A woman with a kind, but distraught face extended her hand to me. "*Can you try to reach around and open the back door?*" she shouted, pointing to the back of the car.

I started to hyperventilate as my mind and body returned to the horrifying reality. I couldn't get past the locked doors, broken glass, and giant airbags that blocked every escape. I tried breaking out of the toxic air, only to choke. Pain and panic shot through my entire body.

"It's best if you don't move – I hear the ambulance!"

exclaimed the woman. I saw the horror on her face as I flailed about.

"What's happening?" I cried with hysteria.

"You were in a terrible car accident," she told me.

I tried to process what she was saying, and all that was happening around me, but only ended up panicking more. Rescue workers arrived with a litany of questions. There was some good news. I knew my name. I knew who was president, and I knew it wasn't me. I recalled the day of the week and watched the paramedic's face grow from gravely concerned to slightly relieved. The stranger stayed by my side until I was hauled away in the ambulance.

I began lapsing in and out of consciousness. I awoke to a young man in a white jacket, trying to blind me with his flashlight.

"Are you with us?" he asked. *"Are you okay?"*

"No," I answered bluntly.

He put down the flashlight and scrambled for help from his crew. I thought I was dying, but the intense, throbbing pain made it clear I was alive.

"Go! Take her out of here," I heard him shout to the other emergency workers. *"Tell the ER we're on the way. We'll be there in ten minutes."*

The rest of the trip was a blur – flashing lights, medics talking, and intermittent loud beeps from the equipment. All the while, I writhed in pain.

Once inside the hospital, I awoke again, this time to Alan's voice. He sounded calm and reassuring – and also, genuinely concerned.

"Sorry, you never got to the gym. Someone ran through a red light, which caused the accident. It seems you were unconscious for a while, pretty beat up, and you have deep bruises. You'll be black and blue for some time to come," he declared. *"The good news is, there seems to be very little internal bleeding and no broken bones."*

I suppose he added the last bit to comfort me. After a slight pause, he said, *"If there is anything else, we'll probably find out tomorrow."*

I managed to give him some semblance of a smile. Here he was, being sensitive and clearly affected by my discomfort. Perhaps this horrible car accident was all he needed to change.

"How are you feeling?" asked one of the ever-smiling nurses as she bent over the gurney and looked into my face.

"Ouch!" I shouted.

"I know. You are in pain," she said. *"Don't worry. I'm giving you a morphine shot right now."*

As the nurse was injecting me, Alan announced to her. *"I'm a doctor—retired but not too long out of the saddle, worked at the local hospital."*

"Are you having her stay overnight, or will you be taking her home?" she asked.

"Home. Any excuse not to stay here in the hospital," he chuckled as the nurse furrowed her brow. Alan's jokes always misfired, but this time I was too traumatized to be embarrassed. The nurse ignored his comedic failure and focused on my pain medication. She handed us a prescription the ER doctor had prepared.

"How do you feel about going home," the nurse asked me.

"Fine," I whispered. I was discharged by 2:00 a.m. with

a cervical collar and a small mountain of pain medication.

Ten hours later, my body swelled in places I didn't think was possible. The color of my skin went from pasty white to a combination of red clay from Mars and lovely blue methane hues from Neptune and Uranus. I stood out from my surroundings so much that if I were a chameleon, I would have been immediately attractive to predators. I tried to focus on resting, but the pain was too much.

I slept in fits and starts and was awakened by nightmares of being burned alive in a car. I was not sure if the nightmares were the result of head trauma, super strength narcotics, memories of that horrific night, or a combination of all three.

"How soon will the pain go away and my condition improve?" I asked our family physician, Dr. Norman.

"Frankly, I'm astounded that you have any memory of the accident," he specified.

"When will I get better? "I asked.

"Well, it's too early to know in what ways you will be limited. Any injury to the brain causes great harm. The extent of the damage and initial prognosis will come from

tests of motor and cognitive abilities. Time will tell," he explained.

It took me a while to digest all that information. It certainly sounded like my doctor had no idea when my condition would improve.

The next day, as I awaited the MRI that Dr. Norman had ordered, I grew anxious and panicky. I wished my father were with me, to tell me everything would be okay. I remembered when I was growing up, he always made me feel safe. He would hold my hand, close his eyes, and say a prayer. Suddenly, I saw my father – not in my mind, but in person. There he was, floating high in the air and extending his hands toward me. I squinted and blinked and tried to clear my eyes, but couldn't un-see this startling image. My father had passed away years ago.

"What are you doing?" Alan asked. *"You need to lie quietly now. Put your arm down."*

"Don't you see him? My father – right up there," I pointed, looking rather alarmed.

"You're either dreaming or having a trauma-induced illusion," he said, dismissing what I had witnessed.

Was I dreaming or seeing a ghost? I closed my eyes for a moment and opened them again. My father had vanished. He had always been a symbol of security and strength to me, so in hindsight, seeing him at a time of my insecurity makes perfect sense. His message to me – 'be strong' – felt reassuring. The fact that others didn't witness this extraordinary presence never took away from my experience of this vision.

The following day, I gathered enough energy to leave the bedroom on my own. I had mustered sufficient determination to descend the stairs. One of the first things I noticed was the surprising degree of concentration and effort required by functions that were once so effortless. I had to instruct every muscle how to perform movements and had to rebalance myself continually. I was learning how to walk again. I clung to the walls and railing, stopping often. I accomplished my goal ultimately, arriving at the bottom of the solitary flight of stairs in our house after several minutes. I was panting, as though I had climbed a mountain.

I felt I needed a nap. Looking for familiar comfort, I sat down on the sofa to watch the news on television, like a normal person. My prospects of getting comfortable were shot, as the sounds only grated painfully on my nerves. The words that flowed into my ears evidently did some somersaults by the time they reached my brain. The voices were rendered meaningless, and people's movements blurred before my eyes. I changed the channel to see if the gibberish presented itself elsewhere. Instantly, terror swept across my body. I felt as though communication had just died, and I had to go and bury it. I turned off the television, disheartened.

I picked up the newspaper, hoping for the best. The words simply swam across the pages, like children running away from their strict grammar teachers. I turned the newspaper to see if I was holding it upside down. I sighed and struggled to understand the extent of my trauma. Soon my daughter, Sara, and my son, Shan, came to rescue me from losing my mind. They had come to help me with the daily tasks that I wasn't able to perform. Something as simple as holding a light object had become a hurdle that I couldn't do independently.

My brain was no longer the master of my movements, my speech, or my perception. The musty smell of the burning metal still followed me everywhere, and I couldn't get rid of it. I was ready to inhale perfume if that would free me from the dreadful smell. The person who hit my car was distracted and ran through a red light. I had lost consciousness instantly and never saw how the accident happened. The airbags saved my life but left me with extensive injuries. The impact was from the rear-right, which generated damage to the left side of my brain. This area is responsible for speech, verbal comprehension, perception, and muscular control – that explained many of my problems.

As weeks turned into months, things didn't improve much. I couldn't trust any of my senses because they didn't represent reality. Seeing or feeling didn't represent the way things were. Typically, my foot wouldn't hit the ground at the moment I thought it would, or the floor itself was too deep or shallow for me to gauge. Walking across the room exhausted me physically as well as emotionally. Many things about my physical world became unpredictable. I feared the worst – losing my career, my friends, and becoming unable to interact with people.

Even sleep stressed me out. Frequent nightmares forced

me to relive the accident. It seemed like the memory of that night was locked in my brain, and I couldn't wake up from it. In one of the recurring nightmares, my college-age son was with me in the car as we were traveling down the interstate to visit my daughter in Georgia during their spring breaks. A semi-truck would barrel down the highway, headed straight towards us. I would wake up screaming. In another nightmare my daughter was with me. An 18-wheeler would side-swipe our vehicle, running us off the road. Our vehicle would tear through the guardrails, rolling down into a ravine. I would wake up screaming, reliving the exact pain from the car accident. The nightmares continued to the point that I started to dread sleep.

In a state of confusion, I convinced myself I should go back to work. I stubbornly reasoned with myself that teaching could help with my recovery. But this went against the advice of my doctors, who were certain that the stress of the classroom would cause my condition to deteriorate. I thought there was no way to gauge my degree of fitness if I didn't try. I devised ways to compensate for my mental and physical limitations. The last frontier was my inability to drive myself to work. Alan agreed to drop me off and pick me up after.

Upon entering the school, I was greeted by friendly and familiar faces, warm smiles, and encouraging words from colleagues and students. I nodded and smiled back, trying to mask the fact that I couldn't recall who most of them were. It became awkward that people I had once known well seemed like strangers. That was something I wasn't prepared for. I entered my classroom early before anyone had arrived. I had to make copies of material for my students, which required a trip to the second floor. I now relied on the elevator, unable to take the stairs.

I passed some people in the hall and sensed they knew me. They greeted me and smiled. I returned their smiles with a blank *"hello"* or *"good to see you."* I kept moving, so I didn't have to disclose that I could not recall their names. I was overwhelmed with my new reality in a place that was previously so familiar and friendly.

Once I arrived in the copy room of the building, I felt weak. My body went uncontrollably numb and I started to fall to the ground. I was caught midair by one of my colleagues; I recognized her face but couldn't recall her name. With the assistance of two others, I was helped onto a chair. Somebody called my husband, and with the help of several other staff members, I climbed into the car and headed home.

It turned out to be an embarrassing attempt to return to work. I still didn't understand. I asked my doctor to explain what had happened, and why.

"What you're doing is comparing yourself to how things were before the accident. You need to begin comparing today with last month. I understand your frustration, but your system needs more time to repair itself. Take one step at a time, and don't worry about the bigger picture," he explained kindly and continued. *"The neuro-testing will provide answers. Patients who have been through your kind of trauma usually make the most progress during the first two years."* He referred me to Dr. Frederick to evaluate the neurological testing, and estimate the degree of recovery that I could expect.

To alleviate the pain in my neck area, he offered me an injection, and I accepted – anything to take away the agony. As soon as he administered the shot, he left the room and closed the door. Unexpectedly all sense of balance exited my body. I collapsed from the chair onto the floor and screamed for help. A nurse came rushing in. She lifted me back onto the chair, and the doctor began to examine me, clearly bewildered by what had happened. It took hours before I regained any sensation in my hands and legs.

Chapter 2
Lifting the Fog

The accident altered my health, career, and personal life. My hopes of finding solace in my teaching job sunk. The energy I'd drawn from my students and teaching career dissipated. The thought of not being able to go to work every day was as much a blow as the tragedy itself.

I found myself struggling along the onerous, unfamiliar pathway presented to me by a brand-new life. I couldn't recall my own phone number or address, or the numbers of those closest to me. Dashed were my dreams of spending retirement days on the beach. My precious time at the gym was no longer a possibility. Over the years, the gym offered me a sense of achievement above and beyond work and home.

In a social setting, I found it impossible to focus. I would lose myself in my internal mental dialog, unable to address the topic and get back on track. I felt mortified that I would drop silverware or spill my drink; if not these, then there were other forms of social embarrassment to contend with. The fears made me insecure, and insecurity forced me to avoid gatherings of all kinds. I withdrew from friends and colleagues and limited my interactions to close family.

For years, I had been the unofficial social director within our circle of friends. I was the organizer of dinner parties, the creator of entertainment central for holiday gatherings. I was the neighbor with the garden that everyone envied, and the friend with a flair for interior design. I used to find savvy ways to make our house look like it was worth more than it actually was. I would balance my time between cooking gourmet dinners and go to the gym. It was hard to imagine myself in a lesser role, and a struggle to not let negative feelings creep in.

Having lost my old sense of reality, I had to think about every word — both in terms of its meaning and application. When words failed me, my speech would be delayed. Those around me would be stumped as I attempted to put together words flying around inside my head. This frustrated my husband and bewildered my children.

"Mom, you're repeating yourself," I would often hear Shan or Sara say. Another frequent response was, *"Mom, why did you change the subject?"*

"Well, I hoped no one would notice," I would say.

I longed for the days when I could drive myself around, and not depend on anyone. I used to rely on my memory for groceries, not anymore. I had to take a detailed list as well as my impatient husband to assist me, which was an unpleasant experience. I thought he was there to help, but often he was busy with his own entertainment, his ears plugged with earphones. Still, nothing aggravated me more than what he did on our last trip to the grocery store.

I was horrified to discover that the cashier bagged the meat with the vegetables. I politely asked her to separate them into two. Just then, Alan intervened and told the cashier, *"You don't have to do it."*

I was troubled by his lack of support, to say the least. Once we were out of the store, I asked him, *"Why did you override my request?"* He just shrugged his shoulders. I knew he behaved badly, and I didn't like asking him for help, but I had no other option.

The next day, I was still upset when he drove me to my appointment. I'd never liked going to the doctor's, however on this particular visit I was more distressed. I felt nothing in the waiting room was comforting, and everything represented a disorderly setting. The mismatched chairs, the bright lighting with its unusual shade, even the messy magazine stand bothered me more than it should. I looked around, only to be greeted by a roomful of sad faces. I couldn't even muster a little compassion for others. I was in survival mode, unable to extend myself beyond the perimeter of my own pain and inabilities. I was relieved when the nurse called my name.

Once Dr. Norman arrived, I rushed to express my difficulties with recalling words and memories. He gently guided me back on track so he could ask me some questions. But I kept harping about my sensitivity to noise and light. He smiled and directed me with one word: *"Patience."* I continued to press him about my hurdles, and again he suggested patience. Soon, I reached the point where his words were no longer reassuring.

"Since the accident, I have very little patience, in case that is important to planning my rehabilitation." I professed.

Dr. Norman overlooked my irritation and just smiled. He increased the pain medication and advised I should move into a more extensive physical therapy program.

To make matters worse, two of my doctors relocated their office, and that made traveling to my appointments more difficult. Since I didn't have enough confidence to drive myself to an office, and it was 30 minutes away, I asked Alan to take me.

"You should be fine," he quipped as he focused his attention on his computer screen.

I thought he had more faith in me than I had in myself. Instead of arguing, I took it upon myself to see if I could do it. I drove rather slowly, much to the displeasure of other drivers traveling behind me on the road. I was surprised when I had only a little trouble finding the doctor's new office. However, on my way back, I got lost. I had no idea where I was or how I had gotten there. Hours later, my anger and frustration were overtaken by fear. I felt so vulnerable that I may never find my way back home.

Still, I kept hoping to drive by something familiar. Finally, I found the main highway that led me to my home. I was exhausted and had missed my physical therapy session, but I decided to go anyway, even though I was two hours late for my session. I apologized profusely, but she wasn't as concerned with my tardiness as she was with my husband's lack of interest in my absence.

Apparently, when I didn't show up for physical therapy, the therapist acted more like a concerned friend; she had called my husband to see why I had missed my appointment. Alan told her, *"She will show up eventually,"* and his response made her worry.

I chose to spare her the details that my husband busied himself with day-trading, and he had no time for anything else. His sympathy for my healing was short-lived. Early on, he put some effort into helping me. Once I got past the tragedy of the first few months, he returned to his old habits. His daily clatter of stocks treading stressed me out as I became more sensitive to noises. To avoid the clatters, I often listened to my brain therapy CD, and hoping what comforted my mind also, alter Alan's brain frequencies into behaviors that I could have some peace and quiet at home.

Like many families we had our challenges, too. Most of our conflicts were focused on his drinking, obsession over day trading, and management of our finances. In that sense, we seemed to be a relatively normal couple. Perhaps I had been in denial, or I couldn't see the forest for the trees. Frankly, Alan's lack of courtesy didn't bother me as much until my accident. I mean I knew I had uncertainties and doubts, but I had subconsciously overlooked them. I had daily escapes that brought balance to my life. I felt grateful for my health, my career, and my family. Since I had nothing to complain about during the day, I had passively tolerated the letdown in the evenings and weekends.

The old version of me would never even ask for help. *"I can take care of myself,"* I would say.

But I couldn't say those things for the simple fact that it would be a lie. The fear in me demanded action, forced me to find a solution that I could have a sense of security about our finances, retirement, and future plans.

"Maybe we should buy disability insurance," I blurted out one day.

"We don't need extra insurance. It would just be a waste of our money," Alan replied with a smile.

"But what if I am never able to return to work?" I asked.

"Don't be concerned. Whether you work or not, I will

always take care of you. You should know that." he said.

His sweet talk didn't ease up my worries, I needed a real remedy, and he offered more of the same.

Among other things, visits to the doctor's office also had become like my own Vaudeville Act. It was the same routine repeated at different stages; my lack of balance and headaches were always at the top of my concerns. When I asked my new doctor, Judy Lamont.

"Will I ever get my life back?"

She responded, *"Regrettably, your memory function has been impaired. In all likelihood, you may not be able to return to teaching."* She added, *"you will likely need medical care for the remainder of your life."*

It wasn't the message of optimism, but it was the reality that I had a hard time to excepted. Perhaps my fear of truth, forced me into denial and look for a gleam of hope that I could put my life together. Dr. Lamont orders two extra MRI for the brain and neck and urged me to return to speech and physical therapy.

Once again, physical therapy became part of my daily routine; it was prescribed to rebuild the muscles that had atrophied. I still wore an ankle brace and used a cane for support. But I understood, my recovery required a lot of hard work from my side by putting more effort into exercising. So, every day I exercised at home before going for physical therapy. Slowly, I began to see some positive changes in my physical functions. To some extent, it helped me get around and do as much as I could, but any sort of clutter at home aggravated me. I suggested to Alan:

"We should hire somebody to help us with the housekeeping, lawn care, and to tend to the flower garden since the yard has become unappealing."

"Oh, you will be well soon; just be patient," he said.

He believed I would be healthy enough to take care of everything like I did before. The shrubs and flowers, which were once the envy of our neighbors were overtaken by weeds. Many of the plants that used to bloom had stopped blossoming, and were strangled by wild plants that made the garden messy. I was so tempted to go out there, refurbish the greenery and give the front yard a happier look. But I knew I had a long road to recovery before doing any physical work, so I had to let it be.

It was obvious to me that soon I would be the one driving myself to the appointments. It made sense to find a doctor nearby, and hunt for a tool to make it easier to keep up with my activities. Sara suggested that I use a memory aid device to help me with the schedules. Many people assisted me in that regard. It's a great organizer; the appointment reminder and the visual to-do list are very useful. I am glad that somebody invented such a beneficial tool. My anxiety diminished, when I was able to drive myself and had the tool to keep up with my daily routines.

I thought going back to work would be a reasonable option. I spoke with the head of my department, and she was gracious enough to let me retry. I felt emotionally ready, but a bit uneasy about my physical readiness. This time I drove myself to school.

It was early morning. As soon as I entered my classroom, I sensed I was losing my balance. My mind wanted to fight and go on, but my body stopped listening to it. Because I had delusions about being well enough to work, I told myself I just needed a short break. But in a matter of an hour, I was drained on all fronts – physically, mentally, and emotionally. As hard as I tried, my mind failed me. I had to scramble around for information, even for the simplest of things. In many instances I found myself stuck in a loop, unable to get out of it. I felt embarrassed; it wasn't a good day for me.

The following week, I asked for backing to assist me with the computer and projector so that I could cope with the needs of students. The assistance made it easier for me to circulate through the classroom, but still, I was battling to manage my class. I tried teaching several more times, believing I needed to build up my stamina. Before long, reality started to settle in and I realized that my progress was going to be one step forward and two steps backward. The methods I used to rely on were no longer reliable.

I had taught computer classes for years, but suddenly felt I had been rendered obsolete. The system had broken down, unable to save or retrieve information in a timely matter. I had to wait for the data to emerge from the hiding place of my mind. Then nothing accurate would come out. The file cabinet of data that I had amassed for years was irreparably displaced; it was tucked away deep down in my memory, and I had no realistic map to find that data. To succeed in my classroom, I needed that file cabinet to be in order. I left my position, and one of my colleagues finished the semester in my place.

The fact that I would lose my full-time teaching career had begun to crystallize in my mind. I had latched on to my job as a primary form of safety-net, only to watch it sail away. I felt I lost much of what had been essential parts of me. My reflection in the mirror became a constant reminder of a sad face. My sense of style disappeared too. Once I used to go to great lengths to dress impressively, and look more than just presentable. After the accident, I had to trade heels for orthopedic shoes, and I didn't have enough physical strength to do anything else. I often ended up wearing the same things — most of it black.

Dr. Kasper, neurologist, suspected some of my problems were related to spinal cord damage. He sent me for additional tests, and later informed us about the results:

"Two main sources for most of your problems are central nervous system impairment and spinal nerve dysfunction. If your neck gets better, the spine-produced problems could be improved. Possibly many of the negative effects that you are experiencing physically could resolve themselves. The bad news is that some of your remaining

symptoms are similar to those experienced by people with MS," he specified.

"Never had MS," I mentioned.

"Still take a spinal tap test to stay on the safe side," Dr. Kasper suggested.

Alan thought the doctor's referral for spinal tap test was nonsense. *"You don't have MS. You were fine before the accident. Your problem is cord compression by the vertebrae."*

I didn't understand medical terminology, and I assumed that Alan did. Translation: The brain and spinal cord work together through a network of nerves. Any damage to the brain or spinal cord can cause malfunctions. A neck injury can pressure the spinal cord in such a way that disrupts the nerves, impairs the interaction between the brain and body. In my case, the injuries changed my reality, led me to experience false sensory perception. So, if the pressure on my spinal cord reduced, it most likely would improve many of my other symptoms. That offered me a sense of hope.

To get the result of my neuro-testing, Dr. Frederick requested that Alan should be with me for the review. We met the doctor in the consultation room. When he entered the room, he didn't look happy, and I wondered whether I could take it if the news were bad. He started reading from his report, possibly to shield himself from being the personal bearer of bad news. I suppose I only heard the negative, and every tiny piece of the information devastated me. While he was reading, emotions welled up within me and tears ran down my face. He put down the folder and looked at me.

"There is no doubt that the accident affected you badly. Possibly teaching isn't a suitable position for you. You must face reality and accept your limitations," he stated.

It was an emotional day. What I had refused to admit now seemed clear that I would never be the same person I once was. That was the most difficult of the many bitter pills I had to swallow. Still I had to ask, *"How can I get better? Surely there are things I can do to improve my conditions."*

I could have predicted his response.

"Time, patience, and practice," he replied kindly.

He suggested I continue with speech therapy, and

recommended a book for me to read, 'Over My Head' by Claudia Osborn. He advised me to go to a support group, something I had been avoiding.

Getting my life back was my goal, and giving up wasn't an option, so I had to face this new reality. For a while, it seemed I was wallowing in misery and depression. I felt helpless, sad and angry at the same time that all my efforts were wasted. Then I began reading the book that Dr. Frederick had suggested. The story was about a young doctor with a traumatic head injury. It was a good book; one I could understand and learn a great deal from. I thought, *'If she can do it, so can I,'* and my condition wasn't nearly as bad.

I was motivated, and I took up some hobbies to advance my mental and physical strength. These included painting, knitting, and working on puzzles, to help me with concentration and coordination. I diligently kept up with my physical therapy exercises, especially the ones to balance and strengthen my neck. Over time, I completed *"Sudoku"* puzzles and continued my other hobbies. I became a proficient knitter and made great progress with oil and watercolor painting. To my surprise, I uncovered talents that I never knew I had. Those activities became my emotional therapy; they improved my brain functions and helped me with recovery.

For almost two years, I stayed away from social gatherings, to save myself from any embarrassment. The speech therapy gave me enough confidence to invite a few close friends for dinner. I was looking forward to showing everyone that I could have a normal life. I was excited about the prospect of once again having a social life. However, as soon our guests arrived, my hopes were dashed. Before we all sat down, Sherry, a family friend confided in me:

"I want my old friend back."

I tried to process her words. Probably in her own way, she was reaching out to me. Yet her comment fed my social anxieties, and my concerns that I would never progress enough to be the person I once was. She was asking me to fix it for her, because she liked the other one better. That upset me, and I was distracted for the rest of the night. Half of the time, I didn't know where we were in our chat. But I could guess, it was mostly about herself, with tedious detail that no longer interested me.

Next day, when I told Dr. Frederick about what Sherry said at the party, he responded:

"Find yourself the right kind of friend, a well-adjusted one."

Sherry and Alan may not have been my rock during this time, but I dared not forget that I had other people in my life who were helpful. Since my accident, my children became my pillars of strength. They have been my inspiration and my voice. Both were conscious of my everyday battles and continued to be by my side with their sincere smiles, to nurture strength in me to deal with my struggles. They constantly reminded me that time was still on my side, and I should have more patience – something I had in short supply.

Chapter 3
Turning Point

For months, I couldn't see the progress I had been making from intensive physical therapy. I was grappling daily with depression and anxiety. A thick haze of doubt overwhelmed my career and my sense of identity. Some days, I felt as if my life would come crashing down like a house of cards. In the midst of all these qualms, it took me a while to realize I had made noticeable gains regarding my mental and physical functions. It was not the recovery I had hoped for, but it still felt good to see a shred of silver lining in what had been a sea of sadness for a long time.

Gradually my energy levels improved, mostly thanks to daily caffeine pills. The prescription drugs had been a mixed blessing. The caffeine prompted me to function mentally following the fog of the narcotic pain pills. But the caffeine dosage caused me troubles with sleeping, which I masked with Valium. However, being in a drug-induced state of functionality came with its own price. Many of the medicines I took only disguised the pain.

Often to achieve the same effect, the dosages had to be increased and that was the biggest problem. I felt I had to tolerate some level of pain in order to break free from prescriptions drugs.

But nothing sped up my recovery as well as the news of my son's wedding. Shan and his girlfriend, Katie, had got engaged after being together for six years. Katie is a delightful person – she is a bright, stylish and a social butterfly. I thought she was the perfect match for my son, who is intelligent, active and also quite social. I couldn't be happier for them. To prepare for my son's big day infused me with a certain enthusiasm. It was a much welcome distraction to have more cheerful thoughts.

Indeed, that was my turn-around moment. I quickly dialed my friends and family to share the news. All of the courage and excitement for hosting and entertaining that I had lost came rushing back. The social anxiety dissipated, and I felt emboldened to invite a few friends over for Thanksgiving Dinner. My spontaneous invitations turned into 14 guests. I hadn't coordinated an event of this magnitude in more than two years. I tried to head off a potential disaster by pleading with Alan to control his drinking. *"Sure, honey,"* he said, shrugging. When I frowned with uncertainty, he assured me that the evening would be just fine and that I should relax.

Sara showed up days in advance to lend me a hand. Shan and his fiancée, Katie, arrived to help prepare the table and make other arrangements. I turned to Alan to see if he would also pitch in, but he was glued to the television. With an intense expression on his face, he leaned forward on the couch, clutching both his knees in excitement. He barely blinked. His eyes darted on the screen as he tried to keep up with the pace of the football match.

It dawned on me then that there was no end to the sports he was watching. The football game would run into a round of golf, which would lead back to more football. I tried to not take it personally but how could I not? Moments before the guests arrived, he wandered off into the yard to pick some herbs from the backyard. He plopped them on the kitchen counter, as though I had time to wash them for him at the last minute. I stashed the unwashed herbs in the fridge, and refocused my brain so I could attempt to pull together the Thanksgiving Dinner.

I looked at Alan to make sure he wasn't too drunk to

embarrass me in front of the guests. It was too late. He was already well on his way toward intoxication. His face looked ruddier, and his eyes seemed unfocused. I couldn't do anything because just then, the doorbell rang, announcing the guests' arrival.

"Hello! Welcome!" Alan said in an unmistakably slurred voice. He lurched toward the first couple and pumped their hands one by one. His movements were sloppy, like a child who has not yet learned to walk.

Our guests smiled politely, and nobody expected Alan to be drunk on Thanksgiving. It was as humiliating as ever. I had friends and family over, while my husband clearly couldn't manage his faculties or control his drinking.

"Where are the herbs I cut from the garden today?" he asked as the guests took their seats and were about to eat. His tone was disrespectful and accusatory – his classic behavior when he had been drinking.

I looked around the faces of our family friends, all of whom looked surprised. I calmly pointed to the herbs at the table. *"I have herbs on the table already, Alan,"* I said with as much patience as I could muster under the circumstances.

"Those are store bought. I want the bunch I cut today," he insisted. Stunned, I couldn't say a word, but damage control kicked in. I got up from the table before he threw a complete fit in front of a room full of guests.

"I just don't see them, Alan. Why don't we just use what we have?" I said as I searched frantically in the fridge.

"I want the bunch I cut today," he pressed.

My temper flared at his lack of regard. I threw him a disapproving look, hoping it would convey to him how unacceptable his behavior was. His closest friends looked embarrassed. They were not surprised, though, as they were intimately acquainted with his drinking problem. Alan rambled on about his lousy missing herbs while everyone else continued with the evening.

I tried to focus on chewing my food and carrying the conversation, but I felt nauseated. I had such a hard time controlling my emotions, and to keep up with the façade of normalcy. I wished I could videotape his behavior, and replay it for the rest of his days, but couldn't think of anything that wouldn't seem obvious.

Apart from the embarrassment of my husband's eruption in front of our guests, the rest of the night went swimmingly. Most of our guests couldn't tell that I had trouble telling stories or recalling memories. But I cannot forget that my elegant celebratory holiday dinner was marred by Alan's outburst. He had his own troubles drinking in the past, but I had mistakenly hoped that this time, things would be different. He couldn't even manage his behavior out of sympathy for me.

The next day, I confronted him about his manners at the dinner party. Conveniently he couldn't remember anything. One would think that should have given him a clue something was wrong – but he didn't think so.

"That's not true," he said, denying that he had too much to drink. He couldn't admit to his faults, let alone change his ways. I opted to focus on my larger battle of recovery, instead of picking fights with him.

I was desperate to regain my independence. Once more, I convinced myself I should return to work. In two years, this would be my third attempt. I remembered all the preparations I had put into my last try. I believed that teaching would help me, bolster my brain activity. Instead,

I was faced with a series of hurdles and challenges. This time I would make sure I had plenty of notes to help me do my job well.

No matter how hard I tried, I was still haunted by my inability to retrieve much from my memory. My failure to remember notes in the class left me physically tired and emotionally drained. I was so mired in exhaustion; it took me several days to recover from one day at school. I remained like a zombie for days. I would then summon up enough energy to go for another round, only to fall apart once I got home. The difficulty that I had in maintaining myself in the classroom took the joy out of teaching.

For many years, my time at school and interaction with my students had been a source of pride. I thought that I had impacted their life in a meaningful way. At school, I was the focus of my student's questions, and my contribution was valued. While at home my answers counted for nothing. I was holding on to my job, to have a chance at recapturing my own sense of self. I will never forget the kindness of my colleagues. They didn't give up on me and covered for me until I got back into the swing of things in my classes. I am so grateful for their compassion, but I had to stop hiding my problems.

I could no longer wrap myself up in the fantasies. To be numbed by the prescription drugs, and bouncing from doctor to doctor, hoping that the next pill or the following examination would bring my old life back. My doctors had predicted that the physical strains of teaching would worsen my injuries. Yet had I not tried, I would have always wondered, '*What if?*' My teaching attempts convinced me I needed a healthier mind to do my job well.

It was never my intention to give up – only to adjust some aspects of my life. A simple approach would be to accept my new limits and to realize that, at this point, I was not equipped to handle the responsibility of a job. I had to focus on my mental and physical health without taking on the burden of teaching. I wasn't sure what I would do if I couldn't teach; all I knew was that I needed a plan that wouldn't weigh me down.

To speed up my recovery, the physical therapist added a set of activities that I could follow at home. She went out of her way to show me some techniques, to assist me with sleep without medications. Thus, in addition to my physical therapy session, I work out at home at least for one hour.

As months passed, I witnessed a gradual improvement in my conditions. I began to sleep better, there was a boost to my memory. I also noticed when I walked, I was spending less time on eye-foot coordination, which made walking more pleasant. Dr. Frederick and Dr. Lamont were impressed by my physical progress and my emotional acceptance.

I felt my life was following a positive trajectory. As my depression slowly drifted away, I found myself spending more time laughing and less time being frustrated. Of course, my driving force was related to my son's wedding. It was set for September 15. *"Mom you will get better by then, we'll help you,"* Shan assured me. Then as usual, he would crack a joke to lighten up my day. Shan has a great gift for making people laugh, even in the most troubling of circumstances.

I was utterly thrilled when he mentioned he had arranged a song for a mother and son dance. *"It would be just three minutes long,"* Shan said. I felt it would be a simple task for most people; for me, it sounded as exhausting as climbing a mountain. I just wanted my legs to make a miraculous recovery by the time of the wedding.

That my son twirls me around at least for one song, and that shouldn't be too much to expect. Every bone in my body was determined to be ready for the occasion, mentally as well as physically.

I doubled down on the physical therapy, hoping to build up the strength I needed to have a sense of balance on the most joyful day of my life. In addition, I had to think of what to wear for the big event. Typically, I would dress up in the best outfit I could find. I'd put on jewelry and wear high heels to complete my look. But not anymore, I had to look for outfits that were comfortable and hid my functional shoes, yet not ruining my overall look. Perhaps a cheerful, long dress would be proper, I thought.

Chapter 4
Illusion of Comfort

I met Alan at a party, and then I saw him a couple of times in social gatherings. At the time, I was 39, and he was 51. He played all the right notes to charm his way into my life. He was kind and friendly, and gave the impression of being a sensible man who could get along with everybody. We both enjoy music, theater, and going to the movies. Alan always made reservations for all the occasions to show me he cared. He told me all the things every woman loves to hear. When I discussed my aspirations for career advancement, he said he valued my vision and admired me for it.

At the time, Alan lived in an apartment. He wanted to buy a house but couldn't afford the down payment, so when he had enough money, he placed a deposit on a house that was still under construction. During the process of finishing the house, he regularly asked for my opinion: *"What color should I paint the walls? Should I get blinds for the living room? Would you help me pick out the furniture?"* To give me the impression that he was serious about us. After the house was completed, he moved in. He did not have enough to get new furnishings. Therefore, he used the furniture he had. The place, though new, looked drab.

The relationship moved along and continued with many promises. Several months later, when he came for a visit, he brought a stack of papers with him. He asked me to read it and tell him what I thought about it. It was 5-6 pages, sort of a promissory note, stating if we married, I would be responsible for the repayment of my student loan, and he had the right to keep the fifty thousand dollars down payment on the house. I got very upset because I viewed it as small-minded and a sign of disrespect. I handed the document back to him, saying, *"If you don't trust me, don't marry me."* That night, he apologized and left.

The next day, I mentioned Alan's visit to my close friend, Eddie. I had high regard for his opinion. Turns out, it wasn't just me who was offended. Eddie was also surprised.

"Requiring someone to sign something of this nature signals mistrust. It makes sense for billionaires, not for us

with modest resources," Eddie pointed out.

"Especially someone who didn't have any money to buy decent furniture," I added.

After that night, Alan never mentioned the subject ever again. I assumed he got the message. I was getting ready for spring celebrations when one night, he invited me out for dinner. I arrived only to find out that the reservation was for later than he had told me. Something else was on his mind.

"Darling, I want to buy you a very nice engagement ring, but I don't have that kind of money right now. I would be willing to sell my car, if necessary," he said to me.

"No. No. Please don't do that," I whispered.

"I will buy you a better ring as soon as I have enough," he said. He looked regretful at not having enough to buy me a decent ring.

I was charmed by his promise. He took me to the local jewelry shop, and we picked out a ring for $850 and a watch for $99. It seemed clear to me that he loved me.

"Where do you want to go for our honeymoon,

darling?" Alan asked.

"Anywhere other than the place you took your ex-wife." I said.

"Okay, it will be a surprise," he said, smiling. Then he eagerly pointed out, *"once we are married, I will add your name to the house, and to all the financial documents."*

I nodded and smiled, believing him. Things seemed all right. I felt he would be the kind of person I could count on. I found a teaching job in the town where he lived and began working. I had to drive 45 minutes back and forth to work until we were married. The wedding was set for June 25 in Chicago where most of Alan's family lived.

Before the wedding, Alan's daughter, Lisa, warned me that her father had a drinking problem. When I confronted Alan, he brushed it off. *"She just doesn't want me to marry again,"* he said, chalking up Lisa's meddling to her apparent disapproval of me.

I talked over the matter with his friends, Sherry and her husband, who had known Alan for years. Both of them refuted Lisa's claim. They assured me the man I was going to marry wasn't an alcoholic, and I believed them.

Almost two weeks before the wedding, Alan suggested, *"Why don't you take some of your personal items to the house? It'd make the final move easier."*

I thought he was right and did what he said. I had promised myself; I wouldn't remarry until my children were in college. With both of them in college now, I felt I had delivered on my promise and I could restart my life. Shan preferred to live close to the school, so we made arrangements for him to live with his friends less than an hour away. I was happy that he could come to visit on the weekends.

I was looking forward to my last weekend before leaving town for Chicago. I came downstairs to relax and have some time for myself to process what would take place in the next couple of days. Alan came and sat next to me. I turned and smiled at him, not really in the mood to talk.

"I wish you had signed that document," Alan pointed to the papers on the coffee table. I glanced at it. It looked similar to the one he had brought to me nine months before – the same paper I had rejected. His act seemed so premeditated and selfish; I became agitated.

I confronted him right away. *"Why would you wait until today to pull this on me again? You had nine months. Why wait until the wedding was set until I had given up my apartment? The timing of your request is suspicious. Cancel the wedding!"* I demanded.

He tried to make me feel guilty, saying that his family had worked hard to make all the arrangements. I didn't care. Then, I realized my friends and my children were on their way to the wedding, and I would not be able to contact them until they all arrived in Chicago — In 1993, the world wasn't as modern, many people didn't have cell phones.

My rage grew.

"Let's just relax. Forget the whole thing, take a deep breath," he said, and poured two drinks. I have never been a drinker, and have a low tolerance for alcohol. Yet at that moment, I felt a drink might be a good idea to cool down. I just sat there, sipping at my drink, trying to calm down. Before I knew what was happening, I found myself in the car going somewhere.

When I woke up the next morning, I felt sluggish, and

still had my contact lenses on when I had never slept in those before. Everything was fuzzy, and I couldn't recall what had happened the previous afternoon. Normally when I planned for a trip, I packed everything the night before. This time I wasn't ready. I had to hurry to get things together, and Alan barked commands at me till we finally left the house later than we had planned.

Once we were on the road, I asked Alan, *"What happened yesterday?"*

"Please wait until we have passed the traffic on Interstate 81," he said.

I felt like a child being disciplined, I didn't ask anything again until we got off the Interstate in West Virginia. *"Tell me what happened,"* I requested again.

"You signed you love me. For my part, I will make you the happiest woman in the whole world," he professed.

I was thoroughly confused. I protested, *"But that makes no sense. I don't remember signing anything." "Can I see a copy of whatever it was?"* I asked.

"I don't have it with me," he said, then continued, *"It's just for a year or two."*

I felt as if he had ambushed me and pressured me emotionally. I couldn't remember how what he said had taken place. He saw how doubtful I was so he tried to calm me down.

"Let's just put it behind us for now, and enjoy the wedding, I promise I'll give you a copy as soon as we get home, and you will see there is nothing for you to worry about," he said, patting my arm.

I gave in to his seduction and put it behind me for the time being. On each of the first two days, we had a dinner party to attend. The wedding did not leave me with enough time for reflection on what had happened during those final hours before we left town. Soon, I was caught up in a whirlwind. I couldn't think of anything other than the next event. Despite the lingering bad feelings, I tried to put it out of my mind and focus on reuniting with my family and friends.

The following morning, I spent several hours with my children, before leaving Chicago for the next adventure. I was ready for a surprise trip and didn't even mind the long hours on the road. Five hours later, Alan started to get tired so he pulled over to the side and asked me to drive. *"Just stick to the route we were on,"* he directed me.

Perplexed, I did as he asked and drove for hours. The signs indicated we were close to New York. I looked for gas stations and noticed they were all on the left. I pointed that out to Alan. He was annoyed and mumbled, *"Every stupid person in the country knows all the gas stations in New York are on the left."*

"I have never driven through New York, only flown over it," I explained. I thought something had changed about him. He had become unkind, and perhaps he was exhausted from all the charm he had to display, to impress me. For the rest of the trip, I kept my feelings to myself, and he drove for the rest of the way. It was obvious we were going toward Canada.

"Didn't you and your ex go to Canada for your honeymoon?" I asked.

"Yes, Canada is a big country," he answered.

I wondered what was wrong with him. His recent behavior was bizarre, to say the least. He didn't make any effort to be nice, even on our honeymoon. My surprise trip turned out to be Montreal, Canada. I could hardly wait to get to the hotel, take a shower, and have a good night's sleep. Well, it wasn't that simple since we had no reservations. I was filled with distress. He always made reservations, why not this time?

Most places were full, but eventually we found a room. We hadn't eaten in seven hours; Alan insisted we go out and have dinner. I suppose that was to make up for all the stress he had caused me on the way. For the next couple of days, he showed the gentler side of himself.

Upon our return trip to Virginia, my mind was occupied with what had happened before we left town. *"Why did you trick me into something when I already said 'no' to it before?"* I asked Alan.

"I will make you the happiest woman in the whole world. I promised that" he said again.

As soon as we arrived at the house, I asked for the copy he had guaranteed me.

"It's too late, I will look for it tomorrow," he said, while yawning loudly to emphasize how tired he was.

The next morning when I woke up, he wasn't home. Once he returned, I asked him again, and he assured me that he would bring it the next day. To change the subject and not deal with my constant questions, he announced he was ready to add my name to the house and the financial documents. But for that, I would have to change my last name to his. I changed my last name, and he was immensely pleased. We opened a joint checking account and a joint money market account with $8,000, as an emergency fund.

Months passed; I was still waiting for him to add my name to the title of the house as he had vowed. But then he told me, *"I didn't know adding your name to the title would cost five thousand dollars. However, if we buy a new house, we don't have to pay that much."*

He suggested we use the money for furnishings. We purchased some furniture for the living room, and for everything else we had to wait. Meanwhile we saved for a new house by cutting expenses — we didn't go out to eat at restaurants or to watch the movies.

As summer passed, I noticed when Alan came home he was jittery. After going to the backyard, and coming back inside he was in a mellow mood. It took me a while to find the reasons for his mood changes. I discovered several cartons of Vodka in the cellar, and also many hidden places inside the house where he could have access to alcohol. When I confronted him, he declared, *"I just drink a little to ease the stress."*

I doubted him more and more. I had the horrible feeling that the image he presented to the world and the real person were in conflict. When I raised the issue of the mystery document, he still came up with excuses. I told my friend about my puzzlement, and he suggested I see a lawyer.

On top of all this, I felt so isolated in the new town. I wanted to cultivate a social life, just to get out of daily routines and have someone to talk with. But Alan found reasons to dislike nearly everybody. So, I became friends with a few of his friends — Sherry and Nina, and their husbands. I found Nina and her husband, Adel, were an easy couple to be with. Soon our social activity developed into a good friendship. We saw them almost every week and sometimes we traveled together. Occasionally, in gatherings we saw Sherry and her husband, too.

To pursue my educational advancement, I checked into what options were available for me. I filled out all the necessary forms, but before submitting them I discussed the issue with Alan. He immediately rejected the idea. *"I'm not your sugar daddy, I don't want you to get too smart for me,"* he said. When I looked at him in shock, he continued, *"I don't need a career wife, stop the nonsense."*

I was dumbfounded by his reaction. His encouragement and support of my ambition to advance in my field was a big factor in my decision to marry him. I couldn't understand the shift. I avoided talking to him that night.

The next day he came to me and said, *"Listen, very soon I'm going to retire, I want you to travel with me. You don't need to work. We have a house, we have a pension, and you are set no matter what. Just hold onto your present job until my retirement in 2004."*

I felt it was an unfair demand. I wondered why I had to set aside my needs to accommodate him. I still wanted his support; I didn't want to come home to a madman.

To take my mind off the frustration, I busied myself with other plans. The house still didn't have any window treatments. I determined that we could buy some ready-made, but others would have to be customized to fit the arches. I found a company to make them for us, but Alan told me we didn't have funds for it.

"If you want drapes, you have to do it yourself," he insisted.

"How can I make window drapes with no experience?" I protested.

"Educate yourself, that's the alternative," he said.

To teach myself how to make the drapes, I started with just one window. I tried to take it as a learning experience. It took me a long time to finish it, but the drapes turned out to be acceptable.

My next project was to landscape the front yard – it was boring. Shan helped me with the design, and we added flowerbeds and flowering bushes. But most of them died six weeks later, even though I watered them regularly, and they had plenty of sunshine. I thought maybe we hadn't set them far enough into the ground. When I dug deeper into the soil, I ran into a thick layer of debris. Consequently, the roots of the plants had nowhere to spread and hold water, so for the time being I had to grow low maintenance greenery.

For almost two years, I worked inside and outside the

house to make it more presentable. When my in-laws announced they were coming to town, I was ready to receive them. I planned a dinner party for them and invited all our new and old friends. It made me so happy when I found out Sara and Shan would be in town too. I wanted the house to be just right. The day before the dinner party, I arranged several bouquets of flowers for the tables to make the place cozier. I was glad that things seemed to be coming together well. I thought Alan would be very pleased with all I had been able to accomplish. I was on the porch when he arrived through the backdoor.

"Look," I said, pointing to the potted flowers that I made. I was looking forward to hearing him compliment my work.

"Don't ever buy plants. They're useless," he told me in an irate voice.

"How would I know that? It seems you keep making up the rules without telling me what they are. I thought you wanted everything to be presentable when your family came for a visit. I guess I was wrong about it," I said, throwing up my hands in disappointment.

I felt my original expectations of Alan had been unrealistic. I was trying to adjust to my new life and develop a sense of comfort. But he made it so hard for me to relax. I saw him transformed into someone unrecognizable. It seemed as if he had married me so that he could be himself – distant and thoughtless. His disorderly behavior concerned me, and so did his drinking. By nature, I'm not a confrontational person and avoid arguments at all cost. When I'm upset, I retreat to a corner, read a book or listen to music to calm myself down.

To understand Alan, someone who puzzled me at every turn, wasn't easy. Anytime I raised the subject of the alleged document, he dodged the discussion. If I caught him in a better mood, I'd bring up the issues that concerned me. This was an attempt to make it right between us. One Saturday, I found a window of opportunity in the silence of the early morning. I set the breakfast table on the patio, expecting to have a decent conversation with him.

As I was drinking my tea, I looked at Alan's face to see if he could handle the discussion that I wanted to have. Gently, I brought up the subject that worried me.

Instantly, he turned on the charm. *"You know I love*

you," he said to persuade me to leave things alone.

"All I'm asking you is to bring me a copy of whatever you have, to put my mind at ease," I requested forcefully.

"I just forget," he said.

"It has been two years, I need the truth," I protested.

He detected the anger in my voice, *"I'm not trying to hurt you,"* he stated.

I got up and argued, *"I wish I could believe you."*

I was convinced I needed the advice of an attorney. The next day, I made an appointment with a lawyer to explain what had taken place. The lawyer questioned the validity of a document that had been obtained in such a devious manner. And legally I had a right to have a copy of any document he said I had signed. He advised me to demand a copy so we could examine its validity. *"Either he will give you a copy, or he'll refuse. If he declines your request, you could sue him—the same as filing for divorce."* He clarified.

I went home, hoping that with an attorney in the picture, Alan would act responsibly. When he came home, I firmly demanded a copy of the alleged documents.

He quickly softened his tone, shrugged his shoulders and said, *"Oh, I already tore it up and threw it out."*

I was aggravated, to say the least. *"Why didn't you show it to me first?"* I objected.

"Sorry, didn't see it that way. I told you it was for a year or two," he reasoned.

I had no way of knowing whether he was telling me the truth. Possibly, it had all been a ruse just to control me. I hoped he was telling me the truth this time. I don't believe any relationship can survive or grow with the veil of suspicion hanging over it. I wanted to give my marriage a chance, so I let that be the end of those discussions.

Five years passed, and nothing much changed. The best part of my day was my teaching job, and to avoid the conflicts in my marriage, I paid for anything I needed. Then Alan suggested we should use a separate card for the household, so we shared a 'Delta credit card.' At the time, most places didn't accept that card. I used it just once for reframing two paintings, thinking Alan would be happy. As it turned out I was wrong.

"Give me the card back," he said.

"But why?" I asked, more confused than angry.

"Just give it back," he demanded.

I had no plans of doing that, and I didn't want to get into an argument, so I turned and began walking to the kitchen. I heard a noise behind me, I turned, only to find Alan rummaging through the contents of my bag. I was outraged; before I could reach him, he pulled the card from my purse and stuffed it in his front pocket. He left me speechless and thinking, 'what kind of a power game is he playing?'

My life bounced between his charm, and his daily aloofness that baffled me. He also didn't have much of a bond with his three children from his previous marriage. He saw them as disappointments who didn't measure up to his standard. His verdict on his sons was even harsher than on his daughter. He wanted the kind of children he could brag about, and in that respect, they failed his unrealistic expectations. That being said, he still loved them, but he couldn't stand their lifestyle. When they came for a visit, he showed a warmer side, but he could be sarcastic if they questioned his authority as a father figure.

The dysfunction of his relationship with his kids affected me too. I had to endure his critical remarks. Instead of validating their emotions, he constantly pushed them into doing things his way. In his opinion, nobody, other than him, could do anything right. He always looked for others' faults to validate his point, and find enough reasons to get drunk. For years he used the same methods to excuse his behavior.

His drinking became a serious problem, and made it impossible for me to live a normal life. I couldn't get used to the odor of alcohol, and his lousy reasons to have more of it. One day when he provoked an argument to have room for drinking, I got so mad at him that I fired back. *"You have the nerve to tell me what to do. If you don't like how I do things, get yourself a housekeeper, I'm not your slave."* I turned around and left before things got ugly.

Another episode that's still fresh in my memory: It was early morning; Alan had misplaced his carrier bag and I had nothing to do with it.

"Where did you put my bag? It was right here," he began interrogating me like a cop.

"I've not seen your bag, you may have left it upstairs," I told him.

He rushed upstairs and came back in moments. *"It isn't there!"* he yelled. *"You must have put it somewhere."*

"Maybe you put it in your car?" I suggested, trying to overlook his rudeness.

"It isn't there," he said.

"Do you want me to look for it?" I asked.

He looked at me accusingly, then he hurried downstairs to the garage, and hurried back inside after a while.

I heard his footsteps and asked, *"Did you find it?"*

"Yes," he answered smugly.

"You owe me an apology," I said, folding my arms over my chest. I resented him for the accusation. Instead of dealing with getting older, and accepting that he would forget things like everybody else, he used the blame games.

It was clear to me that we needed professional help for our marriage. I felt a healthy relationship shouldn't be this confusing. I just didn't know how to get my point across to him. Any time I tried talk to him, he would roll his eyes and busy himself with something else, to signal that he didn't want to listen. He lacked the keenness to resolve the hitches in the marriage, and saw it more like a fixed algorithm than an ongoing process. I suggested marriage counseling.

"Things are okay on my side," he said.

I thought I was doing something wrong, and I had to figure it out by myself. I began reading books to learn about the dos and don'ts of a good relationship. I also gave Alan a book to read so we could have a conversation about it afterward, to see if he understood my views. He said he would take it to his office and read it during the week. Several weeks passed. I asked him if he had read the book, and he said he didn't find the time. Eventually I found the book under the couch; it was obvious he never took the book out of the house. I realized my hopes were in vain.

No matter what I tried, he always found ways around it. I felt discouraged. But when I heard Dr. John Gray, an expert in relationships would be on Oprah's show, and that he would give the audience an opportunity to ask questions. I thought that would be a great chance to watch with Alan. Perhaps start a discussion in that way, and hoped someone would ask the same questions that I had — in late 1990.

The night of that program, we were in Chicago, staying with his sister, Savile.

"Would you please change the channel so we can watch Dr. Gray on Oprah's show?" I asked Alan.

"I prefer watching something else," he stated.

"Then could you tape the show so I could watch it later," I asked him and his sister.

"You shouldn't watch that kind of a show. Oprah brainwashes her women viewers," he said, in an irritated voice.

I looked at his sister, hoping to get some support, but she took his side and was as outraged as her brother. I felt I was caught up in a crossfire. I kept quiet out of respect as I was a guest in her house. Evidently none of them progressed in their thinking, and both favored the lazy approach of domination, over love and respect as a sensible remedy in relationships. It was the last time I ever stayed in Savile's house, from that point on, Alan made the annual trip to Chicago by himself.

One of Alan's obsessions that bothered me was to postpone any spending until our retirement. He saw things through a lens of scarcity, and he could never have enough. He insisted we should save as much as possible to safeguard our future. His viewpoint never made sense to me. Life isn't an asset to put away and gain value, we should enjoy it as it comes, and not wait for tomorrows that might never arrive.

I adjusted to his ways by using my credit card for everyday expenses and paid it off with the money I earned. It was odd for a doctor to say that we didn't have enough income in a relatively small town with a low cost of living. When I finally got fed up, I asked if he wanted me to get a second job, and he agreed to that. Since I was busy with my teaching job during the day, the only time I had left was nights and the weekends. I ended up taking a second job and often came home late. Each time either Alan wasn't home or dressed up ready to go somewhere. *"Where are you going?"* I would ask.

"Out to have a drink," he would answer. Then, he wouldn't show up until three a.m. or later.

One night, he didn't come home at all. I worried all

night. He called early the next morning, telling me he was in the hospital. The night before, he had been picked up by the police on DUI charges, and they had taken him to the hospital. As expected, he blamed me, saying that since I wasn't home, he had to go out and conveniently forgot to mention I had to work at nights. He lacked the emotional ability to communicate sincerely. In reality, he didn't want me to get a second job, but instead of make it easier for me he used a different tactic to get his way.

To keep him and other drivers safe, I quit my second job. Alan's driver license was partially suspended for a year. It became my job to take him places he wanted to go, and he seemed to like it. Still, he wanted me to believe he wasn't an alcoholic. I wasn't convinced. I believe anybody who can't live without alcohol even for one day, certainly is an alcoholic. His oldest sister, Shella, suggested I dilute the alcohol to curtail the effects of his drinking. The technique worked for a while until he switched to something else.

Anytime I adjusted to his odd behavior, then he would shock me with something else. While he grumbled about not having enough income, I heard from others that Alan had been investing heavily in the stock market. I wondered where he got the money to make such investments. A year ago, I had asked him how much money we had in stocks, and he told me around $150,000. In light of the new information, I was determined to find out about the large scale of the investments.

For years, he had been secretive about his use of the computer. Any time I entered the room, he would shut down the computer by finding a reason to leave. I never associated the shutdown of the computer with our finances. One day when he left the computer on while he was on the phone in another room, I took the opportunity to glance at the computer screen. I saw he was in the process of day trading, so I quickly saved the screen to a private file on the hard drive and left the room.

Later when I checked the file I had saved, I was shocked to find he had nearly one and a half million dollars, just in one account. Obviously, what he had told me earlier was a lie. I had no idea he had put so much money into the stock market. Promptly, I transferred the file from the hard drive to a different folder, in case he deleted it. Then, I confronted him with what I had learned.

"If you had known we had that much money, you would nag at me to hire somebody for housekeeping, or perhaps waste it on furniture. Now you can appreciate it. We saved for our future, half of it will be yours. Everything I do is for us to secure our future," he said. That was his sales pitch, I suspected.

A perfect illusion, once more, he tried to convince me he had done it all for the two of us. I was tired of arguing. I saw my opportunity. *"Since we have plenty of money, adding my name to the house shouldn't be an issue,"* I pointed out.

"I will take care of it," he said, feeling cornered.

In a matter of months, the stock market crashed – the year 2000. We lost almost everything, at least that's what Alan told me. Then he said, *"Since we don't have the money to add your name to the house, we could borrow against the house, and pay off the remaining of your student loan, $14,000. Then you pay $750 a month into the joint account until all of it is paid off. That way we can claim the interest on our income tax, and have extra cash for investment."*

"I waited so long, and you brought us to this point again," I expressed my frustration for his delay.

To gain a sense of peace, I buried myself into gardening. I was still digging out pieces of debris from our front yard, to replace them with additional topsoil and mulch. Once the soil showed it could sustain the plant's lives for the entire season, I felt satisfied with the repair process. That at last I finished the project, and I could now grow my favorite flowers.

Somehow, I never got comfortable in our house, and I was looking forward to selling it and buying another one. So, when our close friends, Nina and Adel moved to Orlando, Florida, Alan suggested:

"We should look into moving to Orlando. I could get a job with the local hospital, and we can buy a house close to our friends."

"Great! we are moving," I said excitedly.

Soon after, we visited our friends in their new home. We also explored our options for a new house to buy. Then again, Alan changed his mind without discussing it with me.

"Too many hurricanes in Florida. It's not a safe place to live," he declared. *"The safest place would be South Carolina, but we should wait until my retirement."*

"Okay I will wait," I said with as much patience as could be assembled.

To reduce the stress at home, I put some effort into making the house more inviting. We bought new furniture to perk up the space. I also adjusted some of the lightings, to enhance the surroundings and make the place calmer. To brighten the rooms, I often added bouquets of flowers. I love fresh flowers so I grow them at home, and tastefully arranged the cut flowers for the tables including the kitchen counter, to cheer us up. In cold winters, when I didn't have much access to fresh flowers, I made bouquets from different colors of foliage. Still I felt something wasn't right, I believed the problem would be solved once we bought a new house.

Alan set his retirement for August 2004, and he became nicer. I had two weeks off so we decided to celebrate his retirement by taking a vacation. We thought the trip would strengthen our marriage and bring us closer to each other. We both had a good time. When we returned home, Alan said he would look for good places to retire.

I encouraged him since he had more time on his hands, he should visit his preferred places. Once he found a place he liked, we could go together and look for a house. He agreed but busied himself with stocks trading. Afterward, he entertained himself with TV and his drink of choice – vodka on the rocks. He couldn't get himself out of his comfort zone and into action mode.

Chapter 5
New Challenges

Months flew by, and I made enough progress to feel confident that I could travel to my son's wedding, and nothing made me happier. I was committed to not only dance with him, but also play the important role I expected of myself as a mother.

As we were getting ready for Shan's wedding, out of the blue, Alan had a heart attack. This was a result of the interaction of two medications. I called 911 and took him to the local hospital. Once there, he went directly to the surgery room, and I had to wait outside to hear from his doctor. After a couple of hours his doctor talked to me about his condition. "Alan is *fine, but he needed an additional stent, and he shouldn't drink alcohol.*" He warned me about the effect of mixing the medication with alcohol.

I stayed with Alan until 6 a.m. when the hospital kicked me out. Once I got home, it was too early to call the family to let them know what had happened the night before. By 8 a.m. I called his sister, Savile.

"Is my brother going to be okay?" she asked.

"His doctor believes he will be fine," I answered.

Then I called my stepdaughter, Lisa.

"Is my father going to make it?" she asked.

"His doctor said he will be well," I replied. Lisa was on vacation, but she promised to visit us once she returned.

I also called Sara and Shan, each asked me the same question, and my answer was the same yet, both promised they would come to see us as soon as possible.

The next day, Shan came to the hospital with his fiancée to help me take care of Alan when he got home. His doctors suggested that he schedule surgery for an additional stent. But he didn't want to participate in any other treatments. *"I know as much as this doctor does, I'd rather wait,"* he said.

After week one, he started his own exercise regimen. We encouraged him to have the procedure. *"I'm feeling fine, I will get the next surgery at least two, three years from now when better technology comes along,"* he told all of us, including his friends.

To our disbelief at the age of 69, he actually recovered well. He started day trading again and also resumed drinking — ignoring the prohibitions against mixing his medication with alcohol. Shan asked us if we have a 'will,' or 'living will'; the answer was 'no', which complicated things for us.

One night when we were sitting outside, Alan got emotional. He held my hand and said in a thick voice: *"Listen, we got a wakeup call. We have to write a will as soon as possible."*

Patting his hand, *"We'll do it, Alan, don't worry about it too much."* I said.

"I think it's going to be all right," he whispered glumly and continued. *"The house is yours. It will be paid off by next year. You have a pension, we have $260K in stock, we have TSP, and you have all of it. If you want to buy a new house you can sell this one for cash to live closer to your children,"* he said with a long face.

I felt so sad and thought maybe my accident had opened an emotional vein in him, yet he couldn't express it until after his heart attack. He became so kind and gentle after he came back from the hospital, I could hardly believe it was the same Alan. Perhaps life had given us a second chance to make things right, I thought.

"The only thing I will give to others is a little bit to my sister and a little to my daughter," Alan said.

"That's okay. Why not something for your sons?" I asked.

"My sons never visit me, I don't want to give anything to them," he said, the creases in his forehead became deeper.

I could see him seething in anger, yet I said, *"But you will create friction between your daughter and your sons."*

"I have not seen them for a couple of years," he mentioned nonchalantly. It was obvious that he had a deep resentment for his sons.

"What if the two of us died all at once?" I asked.

"Never thought of it, since I'm much older," he said quickly, trying to deter me from my track. He clearly didn't want to debate the subject.

"What if both of us died, we could divide everything

between our five children. Just an idea," I suggested.

"Good point, I would like to make my sister the executor of the estate, but my sister is out of state. We should choose someone from the state. I don't trust Lisa, and she disappointed me many times," he said, chewing on his words.

"What about Sara, do you trust her?" I asked.

"I trust her as much as I trust my sister," he responded, looking at me.

"That is settled then," I said. This was a sad conversation that I felt we finished peacefully.

The following morning, I called the lawyer and made an appointment. I had a doctor's appointment too, so I told Alan we would see the lawyer after my doctor's visit. He was concerned about his health and convinced me not to delay it, that he must take care of the matter as soon as possible.

"I will go to this session and write everything that the lawyer and I discuss. Then I'll bring it home for you to see and make the necessary changes before signing," he reassured me as he gathered the things for his meeting with

the attorney.

I was home when he came back from the lawyer's office.

"How was the meeting?" I asked.

"I put everything on a disk," he said.

"May I see it?" I requested.

"I've to go upstairs to change, then I will bring the disk to you." He stated.

He didn't come back downstairs, though. A couple of hours later, I went upstairs and saw he was in the computer room, busy with day trading.

"Can I see the copy of the disk you brought home?" I asked again.

"Oh, the market is closing right now. I will bring it to you after the market is closed," he stated.

Hours passed, and Alan kept himself busy in the computer room. It was abnormal, even of him, to stay in there for so long. By almost 9:30 at night, he came downstairs and pretended we never had a conversation about the meeting with the lawyer. At first, I thought maybe he's sad, and I should just forget about it. But then his behavior prompted me to wonder: why was he avoiding eye contact or any discussion at all if he hasn't done something wrong? I recognized the oddness, so I went upstairs to busy myself on the computer, and avoid worrying about the matter.

I turned on the computer, but it didn't start, and asked to enter the operating disk in drive A. I saw a disk in the drive and took it out to start the computer. It was obvious that Alan turned off the computer in a hurry. Something pushed me to follow my gut feeling. Out of curiosity, I put the disk back in drive A and saw the files he was hiding from me. I began to read it, and the more I read, the more upset I got. I thought this was supposed to be a 'Joint Will,' but he had switched it to his, and nothing inside was what we had talked about. I felt maybe I read it wrong, so I read it again, but the truth was right in front of my eyes.

The light bulb went off on in my head. It was like a neon flashlight warning me of a huge rip-off. The thoughts were a splash of cold water, I was shaken with new worries. How dare he pull a stunt like that? He completely ignored that I was in this marriage too, entitled to the truth about my own future. His fake words replayed in my head. I couldn't help but feel betrayed. Suddenly, my anger over years of unmet needs, and all the broken promises boiled over to the surface, and I felt a sense of outrage that I had never felt before.

The next day, without mentioning what I read the night before, I told him very firmly, *"I want you to add my name to the house like you promised."*

He didn't like to be challenged, but from the tone of my voice, he realized I was very serious and wouldn't buy the crap he sold me before. He acted like he did nothing wrong. I was looking for an apology, a sincere discussion, perhaps voluntarily solve the problems he caused. Instead, he became resentful toward me for questioning him. Right there, I said, *"I know you lied. Why did you lie to me?"*

I had to stand up to him. If marriage was about respect and common courtesy, he had crossed the line – and not once but several times. He could gracefully accept the wrongdoing on his part and ask for forgiveness. But he chose to behave destructively. He dumped all his anger on me and gave me no chance to defend myself.

It takes a big man to admit his mistakes. I could never calculate what he did behind my back. This one matter just happened to come to light sooner than he had expected. Mr. Perfect had been busted; his lies exposed. Instead of correcting his ways, he became rude and spiteful.

Nobody wants to be manipulated, and I knew he wouldn't change if he refused to recognize his wrongdoing.

"Looks like I found something I wasn't supposed to find," I said, gauging his anger.

His face was red, and his hands were shaking. He was making no effort to control his rage. *"Stay away from my stuff,"* he barked.

His hostile tone of voice aggravated, *"what else have you been keeping from me?"* I demanded, equally angry.

He looked at me like he wanted to punch me. *"How dare you interfere with my private things?"* he shouted.

His anger was bubbling out, and he wanted revenge for catching him red-handed. His reaction was so extreme. Evidently, he never learned how to deal with anyone outside himself, other than bullying his way. His facial expressions were filled with irrational rage to manipulate me. He assumed his aggression would discourage me from my demand, and that would allow him to resume his authority.

It had happened before – but not this time. *'Too late, he's already lost the power of persuasion over me.'* I thought, *'even charm has an expiration date, and my claim was long overdue.'*

They say who we really are sooner or later shows up in a marriage, and what was unraveling in front of my eyes alarmed me. I got a glimpse into his real character, the man behind the smooth facade. Since he no longer had to impress me with compliments, he resorted to insults. But the more he tried, the less convinced I was that he was just angry. He intended to force me into giving up, which backfired on him. I thought he must be mortified, and that turned him into a vindictive machine.

He began telling people all kinds of lies to justify himself. It was very much an orchestrated effort to spin the story the way he wanted before anybody heard me. His behavior was very bizarre. The seeds of suspicion had been sprouting for a long time. By nature I'm not a guarded person, and always try to find good in people, until they prove otherwise.

We were like strangers passing each other in the narrow hallway, but I was curious about his activity. I overheard a phone conversation between Alan and his sister. The telephone was on the speaker, and he was chatting loudly. When a drunk man talks it isn't easy to comprehend. However, I figured out that I wasn't supposed to stand up for myself, other than be a wife with absolute obedience to him. Yet to his surprise, I was determined not to be silent by the expectation of being a wife.

On the call, he was trying to impress his sister. *"You know, I wouldn't give Razy a penny, and the state wouldn't give her a dime,"* he said with conceited tone.

I tried to make sense out of it, the only thing I could think of was maybe he didn't tear up the promissory note, but I already paid that off. I was so confused, and I told Sherry about what Alan had said to his sister.

"He's trying to scare you, pressure you to back-off. He knows you could hear him. He may not have anything. If he did, he would give you a copy, wouldn't he?" she emphasized. Her husband offered to mediate the situation,

and I agreed, Alan refused their offer.

At my request, they asked him for a copy of whatever he had; he turned that request down, too. His airy, calm behavior concerned me, as he was in control, and didn't want anything to disturb him. Shan talked to him for an hour, and advised him to undo the damage. But Alan never like the guidance of others, and he still told Shan that he needed two weeks to figure things out. This was a few weeks before Shan's wedding.

It was clear now that the conversation Alan had with me was under false pretenses. He knew his treachery would be a deal-breaker, yet he was so focused on himself that he couldn't let go of temptation. I've always believed that most people were kind, and decent by nature, but nothing shook Alan. Even my near-death accident didn't jump-start his sympathy, which made me wonder if he ever had any to begin with.

Two weeks later, Sara and Shan returned home to help me get ready for the wedding. In the meantime, Alan asked Sara to sit with him and have a talk, but not inside the house.

"I don't want your mother to hear us," he said.

Thus, they went outside in the August weather to have a conversation about me, but when they came back inside, Sara was very upset and I didn't know why.

Shan asked Alan if he had changed anything since their last conversation.

"No," Alan said.

"Is 'no' your final answer?" Shan asked.

"Yes," Alan replied.

"I'm puzzled by the absence of all sensitivity in you. You just made false promises to my mother. To put her in a position where she'd just put more effort into taking care of you when you refuse to do the same for her. Your lack of interest in what would happen to my mother just shows how emotionally deficient you are."

Then without waiting for an answer, Shan added:

"I don't want you at my wedding, my wedding is for people who care for us. It's obvious you don't care for my mother or any of us, I don't want you there," he said resolutely.

Later, Sara said during her long talk with Alan, he refused to listen to her at all. Any time she tried to share her concerns with him, he just quickly dismissed all her worries, and kept insisting he was the nice guy in this scenario. He ignored any valid points that Sara tried to make, and he denied that there were any issues in the first place that had to be resolved.

"Why did you say things to my mother when you had a plan to do the opposite?" Sara asked.

"If I asked a seven-year-old what she wanted for Christmas, she would give me a long list," he said.

"What does a seven-year-old have to do with my mother?" Sara protested.

"Well," he said. Without explaining anymore.

His scorn and justifications for himself actually had a broader meaning. All of the things he said clued me into his motives. Evidently, honesty was not a winning plan for him. So, he wore a mask of compassion and told me all the things I wanted to hear to feel secure, when in reality, it was all a set of elaborate lies. It revealed his lack of regard; he saw his wife as a child who must be tricked to get her out of his way.

After my accident, when I couldn't reestablish my life, I had looked for comfort in my husband and wanted him to defend me. That I could have a sense of peace, knowing I will be okay in years to come. He tapped into my emotions of insecurity, and left me floundering for answers. Why so many lies? When he had the key of full control in his hand, he could do whatever he wanted quietly and I wouldn't even find out. Why did he have to manipulate me with such intense emotions? I recalled so vividly; he sat there with so much sadness on his face, he had held my hand and told me those words that I had believed in a somber voice.

Obviously, he was aware of his wrongdoing so he faked emotions to gain credibility. He played on my anxiety, added a dose of exaggeration to sugar coat his commitment. To make me believe he had enough love in his heart to make things right between us. He lied with an agenda, to give me the illusion of safety so that I would never question his intentions. He believed, if I was convinced of everything that he would do for me, I would give him greater care. It was a coordinated effort to secure my obligation to him, without doing anything to earn it. He thought his art of showing fake emotions would keep him safe from the betrayal of his own words.

I was especially disturbed that these things unfolded right before my son's wedding. Alan always felt powerful when he injected distress in my moments of joy. I shouldn't be surprised as I had seen the movie before. His behavior in public gatherings forced me to limit our socializing to special occasions. Still, he wasn't able to control himself.

I could rewind and go back to last year's Thanksgiving. I believed that after my accident he would have some compassion, but he proved me wrong. I thought of the year before his retirement, the spring celebration. Every year, I would go to great lengths to make sure the party would be fun for everybody. In many instances, Alan had ruined the event for everybody when he didn't get his way.

Marriage should bring the energy of togetherness, but he was incapable of rising above his own self-pity. I think the closeness I shared with my children stirred something in him. Perhaps it made him feel he was a failure as a father. His son had married a few years ago without inviting him. Possibly he thought his father would embarrass him, like the way he embarrassed me.

There was a certain way in which Alan handled himself. He could be a good friend to certain people or a nice man in the neighborhood, but he was a terrible husband and a lousy father. He didn't have the strength of character to be fair. For years I gave him the benefit of the doubt and overlooked his blunders. I put up with his heavy drinking, online gambling, and many other things that concerned me. But this time, he had crossed the boundaries, and I have no tolerance for such scheming.

I promised myself I wouldn't let my emotional stress drag me down. I had a wedding to attend, and I wanted that to be my focus. I felt it was my duty to nurture my soul and lift up my own spirits, and not allow the pressure at home get to me and affect my enjoyment. After all, Shan is my only son, and I wanted to be happy on his big day.

I wish Alan were mature enough to hold my hand, attend the wedding, and share in the joy. But it was his choice to cross the line, and it was my choice not to accommodate him.

Chapter 6
Hope for a Little Dance

Shan and Katie first met at college. They were classmates, and that's where their journey began. They dreamed together and followed their passions side by side, and six years later, they became engaged. What's better than committing your whole life to the person you love most? They wanted their day to be as perfect as it could be. And finally, after a year of preparation, the time of the wedding arrived. It was to take place in Katie's home state of Texas.

Luckily, I was able to find a practical yet elegant dress for myself. That allowed me to handle myself with ease, without stumbling in the elegance department. Sara and I tried our dresses together. She looked fabulous in her gown, which was made of silk with pink strips down its sides to match with the bridesmaids' outfits.

"You look beautiful, Sara!" I said, hiding the tears that welled in my eyes.

"Thanks, so do you," Sara beamed at me, she was happy

to see me living fully from my heart.

We had such a good time putting our wedding wardrobes together. I felt ready for my trip! All the preparations were made so that I could handle myself in the most dignified way through the wedding. I also had several injections to alleviate much of the pain, in order to enjoy the wedding without any discomfort. Sara and I also drew up a *"Plan B."* A signal that if I became too tired with my dance with Shan, then Sara would take my place on the dance floor. I was so determined not to use that signal.

I wanted to leave for Texas a few days before the wedding. This was so I could get used to my surroundings, and also prepare for the wedding a couple of days in advance. Sara volunteered to travel with me. We were both eager to meet everyone. As soon as the plane landed, I felt a wave of exhaustion coming over me. I looked at Sara, and she smiled excitedly. *"You have lots of energy left in you!"* I said to Sara, laughing at her vivaciousness. She didn't even look tired from the trip – there I was, almost ready to drop.

I thought a cup of tea would cheer me up, and take away the stress of traveling. We sat outside to chat. Sara was upbeat and very excited about her brother's big event. She looked at me with her expressive eyes and said, *"Mom, this is the moment you were waiting for. Are you ready?"* She grinned from ear to ear. Her enthusiasm lifted up my spirit and made me feel better. I embraced her eagerness and said, *"Yes, I am more than ready!"*

Some of our guests flew in early to spend a few extra days with us. Shan and Katie oversaw all the elements of the wedding's planning. They had some activities arranged to entertain their guests. It was all too much for me to keep up with. But the days went by very quickly, and I tried to participate as much as I could. The rehearsal dinner was next, and almost 100 guests were invited — just so that nobody felt left out. The idea was to spend some time with our guests before the wedding. For me, it was a wonderful way to get to know the bride's family and out of town guests.

It's a tradition for the groom to not see the bride the night before the wedding, until the next day when her father walks her down the aisle and gives her away. That night, Shan spent some time with me, just to hang out. I was delighted that I could share those special moments with him. I knew him enough to recognize exactly how he felt on the eve of his wedding. I looked at him and recalled all the moments of his youth and childhood. And now, he was all grown up and getting married the next day. My heart swelled with emotion — I guess that's how every mother feels.

"How do you feel?" I asked as I fought back my tears.

"Great, everything came together so nicely. All the people we love will be under one roof. Add music and dancing to it. What else do we need?" Shan answered with excitement. Then continued, *"I can't wait to see Katie tomorrow. How will she look? Pretty I bet."*

"I am sure she will," I said.

"We did our best, tomorrow we have to let go and enjoy ourselves," Shan expressed.

Shan and Katie gladly left their big day in the hands of a trusted wedding planner, knowing it would be a perfect day.

The next day, I got up early to find my way around the area. I was so grateful that Shan and Katie accommodated the traditional ceremony in their plans. The room itself was glamorous, with plenty of embedded flowers. It made for a very warm and cozy atmosphere. I just added a separate table with a lot of crystals in different sizes and height, to enhance the mood of elegance. We placed an attractive memory box that included something from loved ones – those that either couldn't attend the wedding or had passed away. Katie placed a beautiful bouquet of flowers in memory of her mother, who had passed away the year before[1].

I wished she could be here with us to be a part of her daughter's big day. With a heavy heart, I threw myself into the spirit of the special day. I wanted to make sure nothing was missing. I pictured the sight of Katie in her impeccable wedding dress and how my son would be glad to see her for the first time wearing it.

They wanted a warm and unique place for their wedding – a historical place to accommodate their wishes. Before the ceremony took place, they captured all the intimate moments with many photos. Of course, the spotlight was on Katie. She dazzled in her dress that had the sparkle of

---

[1] Katie's mom was a victim of lung cancer.

her personality. Her hair was pulled back in a style, and added a little twist to her hair with a jeweled comb that complimented her look. The tall, handsome man beside her was my son.

"I must have done something right," I mumbled to myself as I looked at my son. They looked so beautiful together.

At the altar, Shan charmed everybody with his delightful sense of humor. Sara, as the best woman, graciously stood beside her brother to make sure everything would be flawless. I took a look at them: they were so full of energy! Their happy smiles revealed how grateful they were to share these special moments with each other. They were born one year apart and had grown up to be very close to each other. Both are confident, down to earth, and always joking around to cheer each other up. I couldn't be prouder!

It was a touching moment, when Katie walked down the aisle with her hand on her dad's arm. I took a moment to soak up the intensity of the time, and to appreciate all the good feelings that ran through me at the happy sight. This was the occasion every parent dreams about. I was sentimental to the point of tears – happy tears, of course. I felt like I was watching a great movie, excitedly waiting for the next scene to unfold before my delighted eyes.

The reception was held in the same place, and they had a unique idea for entertaining the guests. The venue had an indoor and outdoor reception. They had staff waiting for guests outside, with plenty of food and special drinks so everyone would have a good time. While the guests relaxed outside, the interior was transformed for the rest of the night. Fortunately, the weather was very cooperative.

When Katie and Shan were announced into their first dance, I got my next fix. They entered the reception hall with such high energy that excited everyone. The vibrations of the music made people more animated than they already were. Their dance surprised our friends and family. Clearly the dance classes paid off – much to everyone's delight! It was almost too much excitement for me to process.

I was sitting when the MC played the song for the mother and son dance. The great moment I had spent months preparing for was about to begin. I stood up from the table to join Shan on the dance floor. I pushed back the nervousness and gulped, as I took those steps to where my smiling son stood to wait for me. The happy sentiments of the day bombarded my senses in those moments.

I felt something lift me up and hold me together. I knew I could dance now - without hesitations and without fear. I can't describe the emotions I felt in words. I can only talk of my tearful eyes, my joyful smile, and the slight tremor in my hand as I extended it to my son. Joy swept my anxiety away as dance began. I was living in a dream, moving effortlessly across the dance floor without a care in the world. For those few minutes, I was lost in the pleasure of this dance, and forgot to even worry about falling flat on my face.

I was so relieved that my legs didn't give up under my body. Obviously, the extra dosage of physical remedy paid off. I survived being my harshest critic. I was on a mission to think positive, and being in an optimistic frame of mind allowed me to reclaim a measure of hope into my daily activity. I felt I had emerged alive from a stranded island, and I could overcome any adverse emotion in my life! I imagined the possibility of dancing with my son, and that sight always gave me the motivation to get better.

Of course, there were still days when the agony was too much, and I felt I would never get through it, then try again. Eventually, my determination drove me toward remarkable improvement. I don't think I could have achieved such an incredible recovery without the support of my children. When I was frustrated with my level of progress, they were there to give me their helping hand and cheer me on to retry. The pain and suffering got me to such a joyful experience, it was all worth it. I will never forget my special dance with my son.

Katie, too, had a beautiful dance with her father. Then for the rest of the night, the party was full of great music. The guests danced merrily to the tune of the night and were thoroughly entertained. For me, the most pleasurable sight was to watch Shan and Katie. They were bubbly with happiness. The room full of excitement made them happy. They had so much energy to work the room and make everyone laugh. Shan was constantly able to find something funny throughout the event, and succeeded in keeping everybody as cheerful as he felt. In many ways, Shan reminds me of my father, and he was a genius in telling jokes. I wished my parents could be there to witness their grandson's big night. I bet my father would dance for him.

Time slipped by quickly. Everybody did the toast and the speeches at the end of the night. Katie's sisters gave lovely speeches – they shared many humorous stories from their childhood. When it was Sara's turn, I thought she would be intimidated to give her speech. But she wasn't. She was relaxed and at ease. Her speech was a tribute to her brother. It was also very funny; I remember the laughs as she regaled the people with her childhood fights with Shan.

"We always made up, though," Sara said, laughing heartily, *"Which is why I am here today – the 'Best Woman' at my brother's wedding. Quite a rare thing, eh?"* She poked a bit of fun at her brother to show her love and make him feel special.

Katie and Shan had their own speech. They walked around the ballroom with great confidence as they talked in a very funny way to all the guests. It was rather like a comic performance, celebrating their wedding and cheering each other up. They make such a good couple; both are incredibly talented, natural, and very engaging in their personality. Their presence amongst the guests made the event cozier and added more fun to the night. In my heart I wished them all the happiness and joy, and hoped their love for each other would stay strong through their lives.

At the end of the night, the bride and groom changed into more comfortable clothes to dance away the night. Shan put on an awesome dance hat to get the party going. A few friends who knew the songs danced with him. For a while, each of them took turns, and it turned into somewhat of a competition, albeit a friendly one. It was so much fun to watch them as they all danced until the early hours of the next day.

Everything unfolded seamlessly. Katie and Shan did not leave for their honeymoon until a few days later. We all stayed at the same hotel and enjoyed each other's company right through the next day's brunch. These special moments are reminders of what is central in my life. My children mean everything to me, and I always wanted to be involved in their life. I enjoy them even more after they grew into adulthood.

Chapter 7
The Breakdown of My Marriage

On my trip back home, an unsettling feeling began developing in my mind, as I thought about how I'd deal with Alan's madness. I instinctively felt that things had a chance of spiraling out of control and becoming worse. Still, I had some hope to work it out, but he showed no willingness to engage in any polite discussion. On the contrary, he seemed to chase self-destruction even more. My demand for truth made him more obstinate and uncooperative. Seeing his defensive behavior only bolstered me to dig deeper to find his motive. I preferred harsh reality over false hope.

Conflict was inevitable. It was a clash of two opposite energies inside of the same space. I couldn't get through the day without becoming aggravated. If we had the slightest of chances to mend things, he ruined it with his venomous activities, and spared no chance to burn all bridges behind him. What scared me the most was that I never had any control over our marital assets. Throughout the years he made many promises, but didn't have the will to follow through on them.

We all want a happy home for ourselves, and a dynamic harmony in the relationship ought to give us a sense of connection with each other. But I never felt the bond of partnership with Alan; I was more like an outsider going inside to do the clearing. I was consciously feeling that something wasn't right, yet I never took enough power to act on it. All I had from him was his promises. The hopeful part of me believed that if I were patient enough, he would deliver on his promises. So, I was waiting and dealt with anything that came my way, still grateful that many other things were right about my life. Intuitively, I kept myself busy to tamp down any doubts. I expected soon things would be different.

Coincidentally, it was the subject of our conversation on the night of my accident. I left the house in frustration, unaware that I was reflexively inviting more harm onto myself. Since then I have endured a string of distressing incidents; from my accident to my manmade troubles. I don't think I've ever lived with so much anxiety. The idea that I may never be able to take care of myself turned my life upside down. I needed to be cared for, but Alan lacked the capacity to care.

Many of the younger women reading this might be amazed that I was willing to put up with this much to begin with. Frankly, in hindsight, so am I. However, in my defense, I come from a generation where I was conditioned to think that as a wife, it would be okay for me to give 'small' compromises to obtain unity in the relationship. But no matter how much I gave up, it still wasn't enough to make him willing to compromise. I put up with so much nonsense in order to get to a better place, yet I always ended up with a pile of unresolved issues. His failure to see my side of view caused me mental exhaustion.

Healthy relationships are about common experiences, not one spouse surrendering to the other. I lived his life without his help and practiced patience to be a supportive wife, without knowing that I had inadvertently shaped myself in his life. I allowed him to dictate my choices, as if he had more rights than me. It was the wrong approach on my part, not valuing my goals and letting my dreams slip out of my fingers. My techniques were not constructive with someone who had no sense of courtesy, someone who made demands without consideration for others. Indeed, the anxiety after my accident was an ultimate test for the man I married, to see if his words would translate into action.

If I hadn't been courageous enough to question his commitment to my financial protection, I might never have known that my sense of security was an illusion. It was his reaction that unveiled the reality of my marriage − the irony lay in the tragedy. Alan never fulfilled any of his obligations. All he ever did was turn on the charm to distract me from my demands. Occasionally, he threw colorful dreams for me to chase after so that he could avoid any serious dialogue. If moments of tenderness appeared in him, they weren't genuine, it was his salesman's techniques.

He is very adept at convincing people that he's honest man, when his actions reveal his lack of regard for truth. He managed to convince me to give up my career progress by claiming that he wanted me to travel with him while, his real agenda was to prevent me from having a meaningful life for myself. I can't express my level of animosity toward him, the way he twisted things to deceive me. Perhaps if earlier on, I had demanded the necessary time and space to concentrate on my career advancement, I wouldn't be as resentful. We all have limited stocks of patience to put someone else's needs before us. Eventually, we wind up resenting them and hurting ourselves too.

I felt violated, I could no longer look at myself with a real sense of pride. Different ideas had been spinning in my mind, but I just couldn't bring myself to formulate my exit from this toxic situation. After so many years of his unacceptable behavior, finding out he carried secrets behind my back marked the end for me. I would rather live with people who are candid and respectful of my rights, than with someone who lies to me. One month after Shan's wedding, I filed for divorce. I wasn't in any position to move out, but I left with no option other than to take legal action to put an end to his tyranny and reclaim my own destiny.

I was at home when Alan was served with the notice of hearing for the divorce. He continued with his day as if nothing had happened. A couple of hours later, he came downstairs and ate something before leaving for his practice – playing violin with a group. When he returned home late that night, I had already gone to bed. But I was awoken by the ice machine rumbling downstairs for a long time. This was followed by the soft noise of drink pouring onto the ice. All this was consistent with his regular habits and very familiar to me.

He thought I was asleep, so he decided to make a phone call. The house was quiet, and I heard the entire conversation he had with his sister, Savile. He conducted these calls via speakerphone due to his poor hearing, which only helped me understand the context of the discussion better.

"Razy filed for divorce," he announced to his sister.

"Did you give a $20 tip to the person who delivered the letter?" Savile asked.

"This is a good one, I'd tell it to her children," he said and laughed out loud.

Clearly, both of them had emerged from the same seed of cynicism, holding grudges like nobody else. On the surface, you would have never known the real character of either of these siblings – until somebody crosses them, accidentally or otherwise.

Every day, Alan continued with his daily trading

investments but ignored the court's notice. At night he chatted with his sister and resumed their discussion from the night before. It became a regular routine. I think the secrets they shared was like a bond that had carried them through the years. Most of their conversations took place late at night, when he was busying himself with alcohol. The endless noises and gossip kept me awake, yet curious about their game. He was bragging to his sister.

"I will fix it," he whispered before taking another swig from the drink. After swallowing, he continued:

"My wife is too weak to go through with the divorce, she will come to her senses soon. I will wait three weeks. If she doesn't *change her mind, I will come to Chicago without responding to the Court."*

"Great, you can spend the Thanksgiving holiday with us," his sister suggested.

"I will, and while I'm in Chicago, I could get a second opinion from a doctor about my condition, to have an excuse for missing the court hearing," he replied.

I could hear all of this clearly, then I had to strain my ears as the pattern of his speech had become slower.

He wasn't aware of the fact that I could hear them, which is why he said something so incriminating out loud. I took note of his artful scam; it reveals his disregard for the rule of law. Hearing this, I made the conscious decision to stay low-key, so I could figure out what he was up to. Playing detective wasn't something I ever imagined for myself, but I knew nothing good come out of a confrontation with him. Other than becoming angry and changing the conversation to be in control, he would not take being called out kindly. He had already exposed his crafty excuses for not coming to court.

When reality mandated action, his natural tendency was to escape on a getaway train to distract me from my claims. He couldn't let go of temptation that not everything could be fixed with more deceitfulness. In a way, he became trapped in his own deceit. Instead of facing reality, he preferred to try his luck with an elaborate plot to escape town, hoping by the time he returned, everything would work out exactly as he had planned. It showed his own obsession over secrets, that defending it was worth all the trouble he had to go through to cover up. I suspected he was masking something more serious than he let on.

Every night, the brother and sister gossiped with each other at my expense. They acted like two juvenile teenagers planning to beat someone up in the schoolyard, thinking they wouldn't get caught. They showed no control over their emotions, other than amused themselves. My first impulse was to respond, but I didn't want to stoop down to their level. I let them enjoy their cover-up; sooner or later, they would sink into misery of their own making.

Before long, his promises to his sister materialized. He didn't book an airfare ticket to Chicago but rather chose to drive there instead. This was a chance for him to transport boxes of personal files in anticipation of the court case as well. Before leaving town, he made a number of trips to local restaurants and stores to stock up for the ride but chose not to respond to the court. He was incredibly comfortable in his bubble, not wanting anything disturbed.

When Alan unsurprisingly didn't show up in court, the judge postponed the hearing for a half-hour to see if his lawyer would perhaps appear. When nobody showed up, the judge decided to let the court resume without him being represented.

"Why do you want to divorce your husband?" The

judge asked me.

"Because of his addiction and his spitefulness," I replied.

"Did he talk to you about why you wanted a divorce?" the judge asked.

"No, your honor," I responded.

"Why not stay in the house?" the judge inquired.

"Because there is too much negativity in the house; it causes me a lot of stress..." I explained.

As a result of this hearing, the judge ordered Alan to pay temporary spousal support. And told me that I could carry on with my plan for moving out. Nothing was more important in the world for me than to feel safe and secure. After this ruling, I was joined by Shan and Sara, who also lent me their support.

"This is our fight. Alan disrespects you, he disrespects all of us." Shan said.

Their warm words that were filled with genuine concern brought me to tears. I know I could rely on them until I gain my sense of normalcy. I am eternally grateful for all the hugs and smiles they offered me on my way out of that house. Before moving out, I left my wedding ring on the kitchen counter – the circle of deception. I also left behind the key to the house – it had never felt like home.

I had no clue what would follow after my move out. The only thing clear to me was the desire to have a peaceful life. I was still worried about the unknown, and my children could see how scared I was. But they convinced me it's okay to be scared, it signals that you are doing something good. Any time I was overtaken by stress; they would distract me by making me laugh. Their presence sparked enthusiasm in me, reassured me that I will be okay.

After my move out, I was filled by the anticipation of what to do next. At first, I busied myself with wedding pictures of Shan and Katie, to renew the good feeling. I framed many of those photos to personalize my space with pictures of people I love. When I woke up in my new room, I saw their faces greeting me and making me feel good. I surrounded myself with things that gave me comfort, and reduced the lingering stress of everyday life. My new space lets me be who I am and allows me to be connected to those who I cherish. Deep in my heart I felt the worst was over.

The best part of my move out was that everything was so quiet. When I closed my eyes, I didn't hear any noise other than peaceful silence. This was the part I longed for, I felt like a starving person waiting for nourishment. I craved to recapture my sense of self, do what motivated me, and let life work itself out in every other regard. Once aligned with my happier emotions; I no longer bothered with the conflicting feelings that I used to have inside the house. Who wants such a house in the first place? A house which made me feel bad – both physically and mentally.

I treasured my newfound independence. For a while, I stayed away from my life's stresses and busied myself in watching movies, hoping to figure out my own life in the process. I was aware of all the odds being set against me. Yet I preferred to focus on happier thoughts, and avoid adverse emotions while getting ready for a tough time ahead.

Sara gave me a copy of a tape of her conversation with Alan. She didn't want me to hear the tape while I was living with him because of what it revealed. This conversation between the two was before Shan's wedding when Alan voluntarily sat with Sara to explain himself. He didn't know that Sara was taping their talk and ended up saying a lot of incriminating things – let him listen to his own voice if he denies its content's truth.

Listening to the tape was surreal. It was like Alan was confessing to a cop that he wasn't guilty, and had all the excuses in the world for all his wrongs. He was ready to get down and dirty by blaming me for all his mistakes. When Sara defended me, he backed off. Mocking me was his way to gain sympathy and keep himself on the right track. Since Sara had not been responsive to this strategy, he gave up.

"Why don't you give me a copy of your so-called document of proof?" Sara asked him.

"This is for me. It isn't for you or your mom," he said.

"So, you lied to my mother," Sara confronted him.

He mumbled, when reality seized the image that he portrayed of himself, he wanted to defend that character. I listened to his slow motioned self-destruction as he gave himself an obvious free pass.

"I never heard such things that you are accusing mom of. I will ask her about it," Sara said.

"Don't tell your mother. I just wanted you to know," he quickly interjected.

"Why do you want me to know this?" Sara inquired.

"I wanted you to know why I'm doing this..." he started and then trailed off.

He sounded nervous, harboring secrets had finally taken its toll on him, but he still couldn't bring himself to tell the truth. To take control of the conversation:

"Your mom and I have nothing in common ever since her accident. Her IQ is too low for me to be able to hold a conversation with her," he said, to make the sale. As far as he was concerned, he should've received a prize for his 'smartness'.

Shameless remarks like that cut me like a knife and wound me emotionally. He had certainly once portrayed that I was smart enough to achieve anything that I wanted in life. I would always remember those flattering words before our marriage. He dazzled me with his charm, he was humble and cheered on my future advancement. It was his good acting performance that convinced me to marry him. Obviously, he had put me on a pedestal so he could put me down later, and exert himself as the ruler in the marriage.

I don't think Alan is smarter than me, even after my accident. Perhaps, he had academic intelligence in his younger days – long before he became an alcoholic. But he lacked the emotional intelligence to respect others. Where I come from, marriage is all about the union of two lives that have decided to grow together and be courteous of one another in times of need. I understood why Sara didn't want me to hear him on the tape before Shan's wedding. She knew that his tasteless comments would've broken my spirits.

Once I settled into my apartment, Sherry came for a visit. We had lunch together, during which she was cheerful, very chatty. It was her usual habit to give me a full description of her day. After she left, she never called back. I was concerned, I called her and left a message. Still didn't hear from her, so I called her brother to see if she was okay. He told me, *"Oh, she is just fine."* I figured she had taken Alan's side, *"sort of I am with him."* She didn't even bother to end the friendship at least with one phone call, or a simple note.

Apparently, she'd come in for a visit to see if I brought

anything from the house and report it to others. I was a convenient friend, but she'd turned on me when I filed for divorce. I let my guard down, accepting Alan's friends as my own without realizing that they're just his extension – like the tentacles of a carnivorous squid. Her actions spoke much louder than her words. As they say, *"If you want to find out who your real friends are, sink the ship. The first ones to jump aren't your friend."* Evidently, Sherry had jumped the ship long before it even started sinking.

During our 'friendship,' we talked on the phone frequently but visited each other once every couple of months. Despite her habitual lateness and self-obsessed behavior, I found her charming. I let her be, accepting her as an individual. She's a talker, and I'm usually a good listener. If she didn't talk about herself, she would gossip about others. We all enjoy a little bit of harmless gossip here and there, but she enjoyed the gossip like a pro.

However, something about her always rubbed people the wrong way. Sherry was going through phases, her fashion sense randomly changed, and she desired to hang onto her much younger version. Her plastic surgery had boosted her self-esteem. A nose job and occasional lip injection made her feel good about herself, and suppressing her insecurities by making herself 'noticeable.'

Alan felt sorry for her husband, and criticized her whenever he was alone with me. He would sarcastically say, *"Look at her, ready for Saturday night disco."*

It seemed like a subtle hint to convince me about not getting any ideas from her.

When I met Sherry, one of the first things I learned about her, that she has to have the spotlight on her. Sometimes a designer bag or piece of jewelry would make her very happy; she would endlessly brag about it and where she got it from. My personal taste was different as I didn't feel the need to impress anybody. I was there when she needed help. I prepared dinners when she wasn't well. I made drapes for her home with my limited experience. Even Alan cautioned me, *"You are wasting your time; she would never do this for you."* I think two-faced people know each other in a crowd, he never appeared to be particularly fond of her.

After my accident, each time I saw Sherry I felt depressed. The things that used to be fun weren't enjoyable anymore. In fact, I had to keep a journal of what I wore when I saw her the last time, since nothing escaped her notice. She always closely scrutinized what others wore, and judged their personalities accordingly. When I was healthy and entertained everybody, she was there by my side and called me her best friend. Once I was going through a hard time and couldn't be a social butterfly, she seemed less impressed.

To shake off the negativity, I take long walks. After my move out, my condition significantly improved, and walking became part of my therapy – as I lose myself in the silence of trees to gain a sense of peace. There is a mystical force in all of us, and we work through difficult times in our own way. Being connected to nature is my way of figuring out my troubles. I feel that Mother Nature doesn't give us just beauty to look at, but it also makes us feel good. In my world, that's a priceless attribute.

Chapter 8
Behind the Wall of Pretense

When Alan didn't show up in court, he got a court order that he had to pay for court fees. Since he left town under false pretenses, his solution was to manipulate the court as a last line of defense. He wanted the judge to feel pity and allow him to file a late pleading. To gain the judge's sympathy he played the 'sick card.' He claimed his health problems prevented him from retaining counsel for complying with the rules of court – a sorry excuse.

He skipped town because he was hoping I would be dumb enough to fall for his tricks and stay, so that he could maintain the facade of innocence and enjoy life his way. If he had nothing to hide, he could have easily produced the alleged document to the court. There was no need to come back in two months with a sick claim. If he was sick as he claimed, he should have been airlifted to the hospital, instead of driving 17 hours from Virginia to Chicago.

The truth is he wasn't interested in playing by the rules. He pulled every possible trick in his bag, to avoid providing me with a copy of his sham document, but the clock was ticking against him. Finally, after months of waiting my lawyer, Edwin Grant, got access to a copy of an alleged document. I talked to him on the phone and made an appointment for the next day. I earnestly doubted the validity of this mystery document that could allegedly 'ruin' my life.

I nervously dressed to meet my lawyer. At last, I would find out about Alan's secret document. I expected that it'd be the promissory note, which he once said had been torn up; obviously he had lied and kept it. When I got to Mr. Grant's office, the intensity on his face told me that it must have been bad news.

"Have you ever seen this," he asked while handing me a document.

My first impulse was the promissory note. As I tried to examine the document, I was stunned. *"No, I have never seen this document before. Is this a joke or have I been played? The promissory note wasn't entitled Premarital Agreement,"* I said. I was troubled by the number of pages. My heart was pounding fast, and I didn't know how to react. I freaked out, and exclaimed, *"This is phony, it's fake!"*

I felt a flash of pain in my head that blurred my vision. I recognized something unsettling taking over my body, and I had to struggle to keep it together. I considered just sitting down on the floor to get myself composed. However, underneath this veneer I felt small, humiliated, and wished to disappear. Yet, I couldn't afford to lose it as I had to drive myself home. Mr. Grant didn't know I was in for the shock of my life.

"Don't read any further until you get home," he said with worry in his voice.

"Have you read this?" I asked.

"Just once," he replied.

"Look to the last page. Tell me, is that your signature," he inquired.

I flipped over to the last page; struggling to examine the phony document at first glance, I scrutinized the signature.

"It's similar to mine, but I have never seen this document before," I replied.

My face flushed with anger, as I began realizing that

Alan's closely-guarded secrets were a written pre-nuptial agreement. I broke into tears and puzzled, how he had managed to make such a horrible thing.

I tensely got home and began reading the sham document. *"Each of the parties acknowledges that this agreement is in and of itself an inducement for each of them to marry and that no marriage would take place without prior agreement with respect to the matters..."* I was shaken, my eyes were fixed on the contents and I couldn't even blink, afraid I may miss something. *"Parties waive any interest, right, or claim to support of any kind... specifically waives the benefit of support rights, including those arising under the so-called 'necessaries' doctrine..."* His imperious voice cut through me like a sharp knife. I wondered who this disgusting man was that had perpetrated this fraud, as I was compelled to read the rest.

"The parties specifically waived and agreed not to assert, now and forever, any claim to the separate property of others based on a claim of marital partnership. Hereby, the term 'marital property' shall mean only tangible or intangible property whose title in writing indicates an express intent to be jointly owned..." Panic started setting

in. My faith in humanity shattered as I realized I was married to a con artist.

They say, *"Every secret takes on a life of its own, depending on how talented the deceiver is."* I think Alan had envisioned the day I would be shocked by the trap he had set for me. He saw the moment of my jolt, when I went through the agony of a meltdown and sadness. It feels so surreal, like I was watching a movie, yet I was at the center of it. It's an exhibition of what he had done under my name. As I read more pages, I felt sick, and for a while, I had to stop the reading. But this wasn't something handed to me before marriage, that after reading the first page to say, *"Jerk, I'm not going to marry you."* Although I did that with the promissory note, obviously he doesn't accept 'no' for an answer.

His creepy overreach before marriage confirmed his grand scheme. He had intentionally done things in a hurry to distract me with the last-minute emotions. I've no clear memory of the night before we left town. I thought I was tired and simply slept through the night. But upon seeing this document, there is no doubt in my mind that I was drugged. Next morning, I rushed to leave town as I did not have enough time to reconsider. He created the right setting for himself to pull off such a plot. The cherry-picking of time and place of the wedding was all part of his arrangement. The fact that I wouldn't have access to a lawyer, my family, or friends was preemptively designed.

Each page revealing something unpleasant about him that made me cry. I was shaken by the complexity of the endless game he played, to take me for sucker. Everything was the opposite of what he was saying on the surface. I demanded the truth, and he made pathetic excuses like: *"Look what you made me do. If you put up with me, you wouldn't see this."* His harsh words spilled all over each page, indicating his contempt for women as equals. Another clause read, *"no expectation of support of any kind, regardless of financial condition, health, or the reason for termination of the marriage"* He sounded so cold and detached, as if he was dead inside, wholly incapable of being human.

The fake document unlocked the mystery of his bizarre beliefs, to those of us he hid from. On the surface, he wanted to be validated as a modern man. Yet at heart of his being and actions, he's a chauvinistic, fanatical bigot. His brain saturated in sexism and not seeing anything beyond his own selfish existence. When rules of civil society didn't suit him, he secretly changed the rules to reinforce his dying ideas. He indulged himself in the fantasy that his gender is superior, and his wife should exist merely as an extra set of hands. The only thing he had to do for his wife was to grace her life with his existence, that she can proudly take care of him with no financial claims. He's that special.

A dictator in disguise, instead of fixing his twisted mind, he twisted everything around him to win by any means possible. His false sense of authority allowed him to shape the marriage for his own taste. He operated sleazily, prioritizing money over everything else, and I became his pet project and the subject of his perverse game. He used a loophole in state law to install his plans. Cleverly, he put together a wish list and acted as he already owned, so that he could later forge conditions to gain absolute control over marital assets, as if he owned them before marriage.

His braggadocio voice emanated from his imaginary empire, where he sat in an imaginary mansion with a lot of imaginary money, buying himself imaginary businesses. He thought, one day, he would buy all those things. When that 'inevitably' happens, he alone would hold the keys to this kingdom. He was like a little boy living in some sort of magical land, not wanting to share his delightful and precious toys with others. Therefore, he made a secret document to legitimize his wishes, then sealed them away from my sight. If he succeeds, he would tell the world he accomplished all of it by himself, and his wife had nothing to do with his victory.

Beneath his well-crafted surface, there is a flawed man with a devious, criminal mind. The way he used the legal system to conceal his wrongdoing required an immoral and lawless heart. He had doctored a document with surgical precision to make the picture perfect for him. A savage hit plan under the guise of a defense strategy. Another section read, *"waiver of all rights to marital assets, even in the event of a loss in career, or disability..."* Those rules that he set in sham document overrode any protections that laws afforded to a spouse. Through these fraudulent acts, he had gained full control over the marital assets as the separate property.

I had never before faced someone so vicious and

deceitful. The level of planning that went into his scheme shows how his mind operated. To validate his fraudulent document, he pretended that two people were involved in his sham contract, when he made decisions for both of us, and it was all in the service of his own needs. He artfully used the word 'party' to tie me to his secret contract while I wasn't there. It was just him and his dark soul, he wrote: *"Each of the parties to this agreement affirms that he or she has an opportunity to be independently and professionally advised by legal counsel with regard to his or her rights...without coercion, constraint, or intimidation..."*

Once he laid out a secret pathway to eliminate my legal rights, he emerged as a caring husband – kept his dark vision for marriage in secret. He didn't want to be judged as a callous person; he would rather be respected than be hated. As much as he didn't want to admit it, he deeply cared about his image and took pride in himself for the persona he signified. Marriage was the product of his wild imagination that he wrapped nicely 'we are in this together.' He used it as a tool to make his life easier and have someone care for him. As a creature of schemes, he even controlled the time when I would find out the truth so that he himself would not be affected by my reaction. He believed if I didn't know about his fraud, I would make a splendid life for him to which he was entitled.

He cowardly built the marriage on shaky ground and put himself in charge of the train. He glued it all together with sweet talk and false promises, hoping that it would last the rest of his life. Old age ran in his family, so he had gotten himself ready for long life, and expected to be served by a diligent wife as he lazed around during retirement. Probably he visualized himself in many winters to come, sitting on the couch in front of the fireplace and entertaining himself with whatever his heart desired, all the while I stood in the corner to serve him. He never concerned himself with what he does to others, it could come back to haunt him. In his vanity, he was too blind to see that what goes up ultimately comes down — like spitting upwards in the air.

For years he was on sugar high, danced to his own music, and so many tricks were in place that I never heard the gloomy destiny that awaited me. Yet in one moment of distraction, he lost control of the train, and he couldn't stop the collision without being affected. The bubble that holds him safe suddenly burst and exposed him. What he used as a weapon eventually led him to get caught. He never considered that his memory could fail him, and swing open doors into his closely-guarded secrets. As if the law of nature was against him, and vital to bring his wrongs to light.

Once the curtain was pulled back, I found more ugliness than I could ever have imagined. I saw a greedy man, who for years had blindsided me with his smooth talk to make things only work for him. His crying wolf 'not having enough money' was part of his addictive personality. He thought the manipulation is the key to his financial and emotional security. His promises were the toxic pill used to disarm me from financial security. Anything he promised to me was delivered to him at his office address, that nobody interferes in his affairs. Secretly he was making good things happen for himself, while asking me to 'wait-and-see.' Which was his approach to have it both ways.

The secret document that he assembled to protect himself from his doing, brought him extra addiction other than drinking and gambling – once he started down the road of deceit, he couldn't control it. He was secretly playing a chess game for two, and used me as a pawn, to lay out a path where I would be trapped to lose. Smart players rely on their own skills and intelligence to win, a cheater like Alan used the tricks to get ahead. He worked defensively to shield himself, planned every move to cover his tracks, and had a solution for every possible problem. If he got caught, he would put the blame solely on me, claiming, 'you signed away your rights.' Given the level of his skills in deception, I believe he had done this before. The worst part about losing the game; I wasn't there to make a move.

During the relationship, he was going through the motions with sweet talk and phony smiles, all while he was scheming against me. He spent years defending his actions, not as a married couple, but as a winner and loser. Anything that might have gone right for me, he shifted to keep me on the losing side. It wasn't enough to preventing me from career progress and pushing me to quit my job. In secret he was taking away any dignity that a financial safety would offer me, so that I put up with him out of desperation. I learned from a doctor, once she told me:

"Alcoholics don't marry for love; they take hostages." That explained Alan's deceptive behavior as it coincided with his drinking habits. Alcohol was an outlet to hide himself and veil his secrets.

All those years, the secret was there with plenty of barriers to prevent my discovery, yet I felt the hint of alarm. We all have a sense of awareness within, but like many, I ignored mine. In hindsight, I can see that there were many odd situations that made me wonder about Alan's weirdness, then I thought it was related to his drinking. I wasn't aware that the silence of betrayal has its own dynamism; it instigates a nervous tension in the surrounding environment that affect our functionality.

Nothing more can separate us in a relationship than dealing with dishonesty. Home should be a wall of protection, a place to go to feel safe, but the energy of deceit at home pushed me away to seek comfort outside of those walls. I found amenity in my work, exercises, or anything outside the home environment. It made it harder after the accident when my financial safety fell apart, and I got caught up in a wave of negative emotions with the agony of the unknown that I felt trapped. It brings comfort to my heart that my destiny took a detour, and resolved my sense of puzzlement that I had at the house.

It sends a chill down my spine to realize how vulnerable I was as I lived with such a conning man. He manipulated everything for his own end. He thought he would be successful; it all made sense to him as he stepped up the ladder, not sharing the financial success with his wife. In reality, he didn't get any of those things he listed in his delusional document, except the house we lived in together. As a gambler, he managed to lose a lot of money in the stock market, but he expected somehow to get it back. Once that happened, he pulled the rug out from under me with no financial protections to support me. It takes a soulless coward to do such a thing. He acted like a snake, hiding in a dark corner, waiting for the right moment to attack.

Not even in my worst nightmare could I have ever believed that the man I married had the capacity to be so deceitful. He crossed every line of decency with his actions, that getting his way was more important than doing the right thing. Evidently, my financial disability started when I married him, I just didn't know. What made us different from the animals in the jungle, that we should be able to predict the effect of our actions. Even rats have sympathy for their mates—don't like it when another rat struggles. Alan never reexamined the consequence of his doing, other than standing as a good guy, despite the fact he was nurturing his actions against me.

I decided to fight him back in the court, rather than accepting a defeat that had been forced on me. To defend myself and pay for some of my expenses of litigation, I considered returning to work. For almost two years I had stayed away from teaching to recover. Since then I had made great improvements – both physically and mentally. The technical knowledge was there, I just couldn't communicate it to the class. I believe I have gained enough progress to do my job well. Much of my happiness had always been tied to my work. I wanted to have some of what I had before, even relatively in a smaller portion.

Chapter 9
Childhood and Effects of Culture

Our childhood experiences affect the way we make decisions. It defines who we are and what we do as an adult. I've had to step back from my life and reflect upon the sequence of events that brought me to this point. I've tried to identify the factors in my upbringing that allowed me to sacrifice my own needs in relationships.

My life experiences gave me the patience and the tools to handle anything that comes my way. Perhaps this strength allowed a secret war to be waged against me right under my nose without being aware of it. I wanted to know where I went wrong, to understand my subconscious motivations, and to make the changes necessary so that I would never again fall victim to anyone.

I grew up in Iran, back when the country was pursuing modernization under the Shah. It was a different era. As a child, I had a privileged life and growing up with a loving family. I have five sisters and two brothers. As they say, the firstborn and the last child get the best of everything. I was the second child, and almost four years younger than my oldest sister. When I was nearly two years old, my brother was born, then he was on the receiving end of my parents' attention. I remember my time with them as early as the age of three. I played along well with my older sister and younger brother, while my mother was busy with the household chores. Soon I realized I was rewarded by my parents' acknowledgment. They welcomed my efforts at getting along like a good little sister.

As the years passed, we had more members arrive in our family. I enjoyed having more playmates in the form of siblings, yet I didn't have enough time with my parents. Because there were so many of us, we learned to share and developed a strong bond. I learned to cooperate, not distrust others, and that was my mechanism of receiving attention.

My parents invested a lot of time and energy in their relationship with us, taught us to value others and not see ourselves as better than anyone else. They encouraged us to look for what was good in others, and reminded us that we all have flaws. They were a guiding force in our lives and expressed important life lessons. I recall how once, as a teenager, I had commented to my father, *"I wished I had a bigger room like my friend."*

My friends' parents and my parents knew each other, so my dad knew a few things about their situation.

"Your friend is the only child; her father has more money to spend on her alone than I do. That is why they can afford their lifestyle," he explained, after a pause *"you know how many kids don't have their own room?"* my father asked.

I will never forget the look of concern on his face. He wanted me to realize how fortunate I was, then reminded me:

"If you compare yourself to somebody who has more, you will never be happy; you will always find someone else who has more." His advice was not to be envious of others.

That exchange with my father still echoes in my ear, especially when I'm off track in my own life. It helps me always find something to be grateful for.

My father was a family man. Playful and jolly, he taught us the importance of humor and a good laugh. A humble man with genuine humanity, he saw dignity in everyone.

His modest attitude carried him through the harshness of life. He was a real estate lawyer who had also invested his time in a political party. He was a big believer in justice and equality in a country that had become extremely polarized. He believed the system had to be changed from the inside out, and by the people themselves rather than foreign influences. He had gotten involved in politics, because he felt he was privileged to have received a quality education, so he saw it as an obligation to be a voice for the voiceless to safeguard them. He was a practical man with optimistic views. As children, we were exposed to many political arguments at our home. It was a regular part of our family discussions to talk about the issues that were socially important.

My mother, by her nature, had a rather quiet personality. This contrasted with my father, who was eager to voice his opinions loudly. Nonetheless, she was still sensible and wise like him. She was warm, soft-spoken, and carried herself with a particular charm. Her life was devoted to her family, and her kids were always very dear to her heart. As far back as I remember, she never liked drawing attention to herself. However, she would support my father in his endeavors to get plenty of attention by being funny. I recall how on many occasions at parties, my mother would sit graciously with a smile on her face in order to allow my father to shine with his witty jokes and interesting stories.

I will never forget my father's hearty laughter. His humor brought a lot of joy to my childhood. Being with him you were guaranteed to be entertained. He could easily get a laugh out of anyone; indeed, there was often competition among family members to see who could tell the best joke. That brought so much delight and energy to our gatherings. Spring is my favorite season and the Persian New Year starts on the first day of spring. Every spring gathering renew the good feelings I shared with them.

One of my finest memories is the time every summer I had spent with my grandparents. It was a great place to explore the ordinary environment, yet that satisfied my curiosity. Of particular interest to me were the stories about Russian spies, that I heard from people who lived through the nightmare of intimidation by Russian soldiers. These stories instilled in me a sense of my family's history.

As a matter of fact, the Russian Embassy was located just across the street from where my grandparents lived. It was a mysterious building that sat on one corner of the street. The only sign of life in the building was a guard with a big dog. Once in a while, he would come out with his dog to go somewhere, and tended to keep it to himself. He never talked to anyone and always had a hat on that covered most of his face that fueled my sense of curiosity.

My grandmother always kept a wary eye on him, and warned me not to get too close to the Russian Embassy[2]. She explained that they used it as a center for spies to meet, and when she was younger, the embassy used to have a steady stream of visitors waiting outside in the gazebo. From front door of her house, she showed me a big gazebo outside that building. Apparently, Russian secret agents used to sit in the gazebo, before going inside the building. She had many stories to tell that galvanized my curiosity. I realized while the Russians were spying on people; my grandmother was spying on them.

It's a humbling reminder, that I had a safe environment

---

[2] In early 19 century, Russian had big influence on Iran, and kept their embassy open for another 90 years. In June 1941, when Hitler invaded Russia, Iran's railroad used for essential supplies from the Gulf to Russia.

to grow up in. I'm deeply indebted to them for having enhanced my life by providing me with a sense of comfort and security. I eventually became the child that kept the peace in the family, and my role stayed the same even when I grew older. I was the gatekeeper for my older sister and the confidante to my brothers in their teenage years. Sometimes, I myself got in trouble because of defending their actions.

Those values remained with me throughout my life. I see my parents in everything I do. I got my trusting gene from my mother and my optimistic outlook from my father. I learned from him to channel my negative feelings into something more enjoyable. My relationship with nature is also a learned habit from my parents, who regularly worked in the garden in their spare time. I will always remember them for the nuggets of wisdom they constantly shared with us when we were growing up.

Once I grew older, I gained my parents' respect, they began calling me their most responsible child, and their faith in me meant a lot. They never turned a blind eye to what I was doing, yet allow me to have my way, all because I never let them down. That affected many of my choices in life. The following story shows the level of trust my parents had in me, to let me stand for what was right. I simply practiced what I learned from them.

I was in my last year of high school, when I got transferred from a private school to a public school. This was to allow me to spend more time with my friends and cousins before we all got ready for college. It was my first day in the new school and I felt out of place - wearing a gray uniform with a white lace neckline and a white belt, instead of the skirt and white blouse that I used to wear in my old school. As I entered the classroom, I became overwhelmed, there wasn't enough light to see where I was going, so I tensely sat on the first chair I could find in the class.

There were too many students in the room and I didn't know anyone there. While I waited for my new teacher to arrive, I looked at my classmates to see if they were as worried as I was. Before long, a tall man with a serious expression entered the classroom. We all promptly stood up, and he instructed, *"Good morning, have a seat. Take your notebooks out."* At once, he started writing on the blackboard. I immediately start copying everything he was writing.

As I was trying to keep up, a girl next to me asked for a pencil and I looked into my bag to find an extra pencil. While I was doing this, I heard the teacher say, *"You, stand up."* We all looked at him to see who he was pointing out.

A couple of students stood up voluntarily, and each time he said, *"Not you again... no, not you either."* I finally stood up, and he asked, *"why did you laugh?"*

"Sorry, I didn't laugh. I was just looking for a pencil," I replied. I heard a hissing sound emanating from the students. I felt so uncomfortable that I had to explain the circumstances.

"You apologize for that right now, otherwise leave the room," he demanded.

With all the surprised eyes zooming at me, I packed my stuff and left the classroom. As I was sitting down outside, waiting for my next class, our principal showed up.

"What are you doing outside? Why aren't you in the class?" she asked.

"My teacher said I laughed in the class, even though I

didn't, and he wanted me to apologize for something I didn't do," I explained.

"Well, be a good girl, go to your class, and tell your teacher you are sorry. You have to get ready for your diploma this year," she instructed, and looked at me as if I would follow her instructions and march towards my math class.

I looked her in the eye and said, *" I didn't laugh. I don't even know anybody in the class to laugh with."*

That day, the principal sent a note to my parent, explaining the situation. The fact that I couldn't go to this particular class until I apologized to the teacher was absurd.

"Did you laugh in the class?" my mother asked.

"No, I didn't. I tried to be on my best behavior today, my nerves were too tense for me to even be capable of laughing. I was just looking for a pencil, and my head was down," I responded.

"It would not kill you if you apologize," my mother pointed out with distress.

"Do you want me to apologize for something I didn't

do?" I asked.

"Yes, for your own good. Even if you didn't, this is your last year," my mother explained.

"You probably wouldn't have laughed when you are nervous," my father said from the other side of the room, looking at me. Suddenly he turned to my mom. *"I will go to school tomorrow to find out why this teacher reacted this way on her first day of school,"* he told my mother with concern in his voice.

"This teacher will monitor and grade the finals," my mother said, trying to convince my father not to make a fuss over it, even though he had a worried look on his face.

"This is a very important year for you. If you don't go to class, we have to hire a good teacher to tutor you in order to get you ready for the exam at the end of the year," my mother insisted.

I knew my parents believed me; otherwise, they would have forced me to apologize to the teacher. Immediately after this exchange, they started looking for a good teacher with experience who would work with me to catch up with the rest of the class. My brother had mentioned that his teacher in math class was very good, and my parents hired him to help me with the subject. I was good with math before, but I still had to study harder, to have an excellent grade in my final exam in case the teacher was out to take revenge on me. I would have to have plenty of room to account for these extraordinary circumstances. Thanks to all my efforts, I was able to overcome all these hurdles and get my diploma. Now that I finally had it, I was ready for college.

To my surprise, I managed to figure out what the laughing issue was all about. Allegedly, this was a common practice among teachers. It was to set an example for other students in order to keep the class quiet for the rest of the year. Since I was from a private school, the teacher assumed I was a spoil teenager. He chose me to set an example for others to make sure everybody knows, *"he's the boss."* It was all about maintaining his own image, without caring about anyone else's feelings, including mine.

My heart is filled with many fond memories of that place, and I still carry those recollections with me. In 1978, we left the country with my husband and our two small children. It was to advance our education in the United States, and once we had accomplished that, our plan was to return home. It was an expensive move for us, but we budgeted for five years. At the time, Iran was still ruled by a king — the second Shah of the Pahlavi dynasty. The country was progressing tremendously. The cities were full of new development with fresh ideas, and several exciting projects underway. While optimism was buzzing among certain segments of the country, many others felt abandoned by the system and unable to pay for their basic needs.

Soon we arrived in the US, protests broke out in Iran[3], and the situation there became deeply unstable. It was a year before the fall of the Shah - the King, son of Reza Shah. We were fearful about the security of our family back home, which imposed great stress on our marriage – financially and emotionally. I realized that many of our

---

[3] Iran used to be called Persia. For centuries known for ancient history, its pleasant cultural achievements. Particularly in poetry with Poets such as: Khayyam, Rumi, Hafiz, Sadie, and many more.

In 1935, name of country changed from Persia to Iran by Reza Shah.

plans had been ruined, and we had to come up with a different resolution and rethink our strategy.

Fortunately, our kids were too young to understand the gravity of what we were going through. We were very sad about what had happened, yet we could do nothing about it. The country was in the middle of war with Iraq and wasn't a safe place to return. The decision was the hardest thing I've ever had to do. When I looked back, the memory of that day when I said goodbye to my family, in anticipation of returning in five years still gets to me and brings me many tears. I had no idea the country I left behind would be changed forever.

The challenges of long-term life in the US became far more extensive than what we had bargained for. We tried to make the marriage work, but it wasn't meant to be. Eventually, we separated and our two children stayed with me. Living in a different country without knowing what to expect was difficult. Especially as I was raising two youngsters far away from the support of my family, who lived across oceans. Honestly, I wasn't prepared for such a responsibility, but I tried not to show how scared I was.

However, the encounters of everyday life forced me to

be strong, and not let uncertainty frighten me. To some extent, it matured me out of necessity. I felt it was my duty as a mother to provide them with an opportunity. Perhaps, living in a different culture brought me a sense of adventure, where I welcomed the challenges hurled my way. I had to make a workable plan that allowed me to handle my newfound obligations. To gain a sense of security, I was enrolled in college while continued working.

Being in an inspiring environment and interacting with young people, sparked a desire in me to become a teacher, and set a long-term goal of obtaining a Ph.D. I was aware of the number of sacrifices that were necessary on the part of my kids to accomplish that. With them in mind, I planned to press on with my objectives. Luckily, I was surrounded by lots of good friends, which helped me cultivate a healthy social life, and have a safe place to raise my children.

In 2001, unexpectedly, my father passed away from a heart attack. He died very much on his own terms, surrounded by his family. All of my brothers and sisters were with him at the hospital, except me. It deeply saddened me to not be there for him. I wished I could see him one more time and thank him for being such a good father. Losing someone we really love is hard. I had cherished my father all my life, and a lot of things I do were significantly inspired by him. I gained more respect for him as I got older, and appreciated his strong sense of compassion for others. He was a man of strength and had a great capacity to love. In all of my dreams, he's a constant symbol of security. I was under the impression that every man has his qualities.

Shortly after my father's passing, my mother became ill. I felt I would never be able to forgive myself if my mother died before I was able to see her again. I took a semester off, I wanted to be there for the one-year anniversary of my father's passing, and I needed to see the rest of my family. It was an emotional visit, and I can't describe the intensity of how we all felt when we saw each other after twenty-four years. We all get overwhelmed with the reactions of seeing each other, and cried out of excitement. No words can explain my level of delight when I saw my mother. I will never forget the way she greeted me with her beautiful smile and loving face. My heart filled with the joy of belonging; we had so much affection in our hearts and so little time to share all of it with one another.

When my father had passed away, I don't think I ever really took the time to process his loss, until I got to his grave. Once I saw his headstone, I was so overwhelmed with emotion that I cried uncontrollably. It was my chance to process my grief. I will honor him in my heart till my last day on earth. I wish I could carry on his strength and joy for life no matter how grim life gets.

For the rest of my trip I spent time with my family. We stopped over in places where I came across familiar paths, when back in the day we shared our time together as a family. I was fascinated by the natural beauty of that area. Fortunately, the northern part of the country still remained lush and green.[4] The constant rain and warm winds made everything growing; it was just the way I remembered. This was the area we grow up in, and we had so many picnics all around this place that brought me many good memories. To say goodbye once again was painful, especially to my mother since I didn't know if she would be there when I visited again.

---

[4] located near the southern shores of the Caspian Sea.

After I looked at my past experiences, I was able to understand the thought processes that affect my relationship choices. As an observer, I realized while I was growing up, we were surrounded with family members that they showed care for one another, and we bond by trusting each other. I learned that establishing alliances resulted in true teamwork and the emergence of reliability. I always find something good when identifying people, and this mindset dictated my decisions.

It worked with anybody who came into my life, until my luck ran out and Alan showed up, who was someone with a different experience. He told me that his parents had originally come from Russia, but he grew up in Iran. Then in the 1960s, he had moved to the United States. He charmed me with his optimistic view of life as if he was just like me, to give me an impression of goodwill. Then, he took me for a delusional ride of our future together, to perpetuate a false sense of security. We all want to be aligned with those who are like us. Little did I know that he was planting the seed of deception, portraying himself as a garden of goodness so that he could more easily betray me.

If a person's life during their adulthood is an indication

of what happened during their childhood. Then what caused Alan to become a snake oil salesman? He was absolutely charming on the outside, but thoroughly deceitful inside. He always walked around with a smirk on his face, while he secretly like a wicked child planned to hurt someone — what a selfish brat he became. He lives in the real-world with a childish fantasy that he can run over others by tricking them. Something must have transpired in his formative years for him to act this way in adulthood. His oldest sister told me their father was abusive and they grew up in a chaotic home. Probably the drama of his past steered him into a dysfunctional life as an adult. Anyone close to him pays the price for their ignorance of his toxic upbringing.

My experience shaped my perceptions, believing that most people do the right thing. But Alan wasn't most people, he perceived the world differently, and I was repeating a behavior pattern that was natural to me. Any time I couldn't solve an issue through compromise, I resolved it by caving in to gain his support. Without realizing a harmful element in the relationship would emerge that make me vulnerable to financial ruin.

It has been proven that academic success doesn't deliver common sense. Any unstable person has the potential to hurt others and get a college degree. Those two things are not mutually exclusive. Alan lacked the emotional intelligence to have sympathy for others. He observes things through the lens of greed, and turned every situation into a manifestation of emotional and financial gain for himself. He virtually tricked his way into outsmarting others. What he says on the surface is just a game; his innate tendency dictates his actions. I wasn't brought up to be pushed over, yet he did it covertly. He used my act of goodwill against me, my compassion and tolerance become the weapons to disarm me and take away my financial security.

There is no excuse for being robbed, but I let him into my life, it was a risk I shouldn't have taken. Relationships thrive in kindness, cooperation, and mutual respect, yet he did the exact opposite of all those attributes. He wasn't mature enough to deal with our life together, so ran the marriage through artifice to avoid responsibility.

Chapter 10
Fight for Justice

Soon we got our hands on the alleged document, we hired a forensic examiner to test and investigate the signatures. Meanwhile I got ready for my legal battle to handle the pressure of a courtroom, and deal with the barrage of insults that were sure to come. Mr. Grant warned me. *"They may get dirty in the courtroom to muddy the water and distract the judge. So, expect bizarre behaviors as they may attack you, but don't let them get to you."* He paused to emphasize his point. *"We have to choose our battles as we aren't dealing with a rational person."*

Based on his experience in a couple of depositions, he recognized Alan's manipulative nature and his disregard for the truth. He was convinced that he broke the law and then covered up his tracks.

My stepdaughter, Lisa, told me that her father was pressuring her to testify against me. When I was living with her dad, she used to come for dinner every Sunday with her little girl, Zena. Lisa didn't want to testify, *"I don't know anything about the case,"* she told her dad.

"I will tell you what to say," her dad responded.

"Okay, I will tell the judge you told me what to say based on our 'experiences," she protested.

Alan didn't like her response and decided he needed to take drastic measures. Out of the blue, he dangled money in her face to shore up her support.

"You know, I've got this account balance of more than $200,000. It would be all yours," he coaxed her.

"Okay, but I will still tell the judge you told me what to say," she persisted. Lisa was adamant about showing her objection to his devious demand.

Lisa knows her dad is a manipulator - she had many stories to tell to that effect. One of these stories that affected her deeply as a young child was during their yearly family trip to the beach. Then when they got there, her dad would flirt with other women right in front of her mother, and play with their kids instead of his own kids. *What was the point of taking us to the beach, then ignoring us,"* Lisa expressed. Sacrificing his own family's emotional wellbeing for the admiration of strangers seemed like a selfish thing to do. I personally could relate to that.

Finally, after nine months of depositions and information gathering, the court allowed both sides to put on evidence concerning the validity and enforceability of the alleged document. When I walked into the courtroom, I felt a wave of anxiety tighten my stomach, unnerving me. Before I sat down, I looked around and glanced at Alan's icy face; he was sitting there like he had done nothing wrong. Managing optics like that was a part of his package of well-organized lies to fool people.

My lawyer argued first, *"that the alleged premarital agreement is unenforceable under Va. Code Ann. 20-151 (1950, as amended), and void and unenforceable based upon principles of fraud."* He made a moral and ethical argument, questioning the circumstances surrounding the execution of the document. As he pointed out, it was so evident that the husband had signed this document just a couple of days earlier to legalize it, and there was no mechanism to prevent him from switching documents, or get the last page from another unrelated document. This could have been easily accomplished since the notary page had neither a description of the document being signed nor the name of a lawyer or law firm. Oddly, nobody has any record of his document except himself and his niece.

When Alan took the stand, promising to *"tell the truth, the whole truth, nothing but the truth, so help me God,"* he immediately commenced with the lies and fake emotions to get attention. He played the victim, despite the fact that he was the one who victimized others. It was obvious that he had come to the court to play the game of, 'poor me,' to buy sympathy. I knew he would cry if necessary, not for the loss of the marriage, but in order to influence the judge's decision.

He started the music by expressing insincere sentiments and speaking in a low voice as if he was on the verge of crying. *"Would you like a tissue?"* his lawyer had asked. He opened his mouth but stumbled into self-pity to make everybody feel sorry for him. He was trying to be victorious for his sake, and he was using the phony tears of 'being on the verge of destruction' to attain it. This was intended to mislead the court, just as he had done with me for years.

In his depositions, Alan said he had two copies of the alleged document and both in his possession. Since then, he had fired his first lawyer and altered his story after he hired a new lawyer, Adam Duncan. Now he was telling the court he had three copies of the alleged document. He had created a number of inconsistencies in his testimony, but once Mr. Grant's questioning began, his story fell apart in cross-examination.

Q. "Do you recall testifying on Sunday, June 20? You relaxed, and you packed for your trip. You were planning on leaving early Tuesday morning, June 22, to drive to Chicago. But then on Monday, June 21, you raised an issue of an agreement. Is that correct?"

A. "Yes," he nodded his head.

Q. "And what you actually put in front of her was an agreement that was not one of these agreements, but was something that you had put before her approximately nine months prior to the marriage itself."

A. "No. It was... basically was the same thing, but had a few changes."

Q. "Then, you gave her some wine on that day. You drink some wine yourself? Do you drink?"

A. "I drink, probably..."

Q. "At home, you don't drink a lot of Vodka? Yes or no."

A. "I had some Vodkas, mainly for the parties. We used to entertain a lot at home."

Q. "You didn't drink? Yourself didn't drink?"

A. "Depends, you know, on how you define drinking. I wouldn't label myself an alcoholic..."

Q. "And you allege that this signing occurred in the afternoon, and you allege that you made the photocopies at your office?"

A. "Yes, I made two copies."

Q. "Did she go with you when doing this?"

A. "She did not come with me, stayed at home."

Q. "Then, when did you give her a copy of that?"

A. "I gave her the copy... I made two Xerox."

Q. "The truth is that you never gave her a copy of this document."

A. "No, I gave her a copy of the original."

He resorted to bogus story-telling to amuse himself, and

couldn't remember when and where he gave that testimony.

Q. "I thought you said in the deposition that you gave the other original to your lawyer, but you are now claiming you gave her a photocopy.... Is that what you are saying?"

A. "I gave her a photocopy, as well as the original."

Q. "In your deposition when you were under oath, you said that one of these originals was in your lawyer's office, and you kept the other two-originals. You were asked what you did with the other two originals, and this is what you had told us in response. Please read your answer."

A. "I sent one to my niece and kept one for myself."

Q. "Okay, and so your testimony is that you gave her at least one copy of the agreement, correct?"

A. "Yes."

Q. "You have never told anyone else that you didn't give her a copy of it, have you?"

A. "No, I haven't."

After this, Mr. Grant turned to the judge.

Mr. Grant: "Your Honor... I have some impeachment here. I have got some audio I need to play, and I need to set some speakers up to play a DVD."

Judge: "Go ahead."

Mr. Grant had the devices set up and began playing.

Q. "Is that your voice?"

A. "That's my voice, yes."

Tape of Alan's conversation with Sara playing

Sara: "So you have a prenuptial agreement and you wouldn't give her a copy..."

Alan: "This is something for me, the agreement is not for your mother. It's for me."

Sara: "She has a copy of it, right?"

Alan: "I don't know if I gave her a copy."

Sara: "You made a prenuptial agreement without giving her a copy?

Alan: "I may have done that," he said with a clear slyness in his voice.

Q. "You said 'I may' have not given her a copy... that's what you said, correct?"

Judge: "He already said it's his voice."

Q. "Well, you first said that you don't know whether you gave her a copy or not?"

A. "This was a long discussion and things are being taken out of context. Play the whole thing if you have it." He was clearly agitated that he got caught lying.

Judge: "It's in the record. I'm running the show, so be quiet and answer the question that you are asked."

As the court's proceedings progressed, I saw how easily Alan switched to a different person. Sometimes, he was on the verge of tears; other times, he became a cold, arrogant man.

Q. "You didn't disclose anything specific, did you? Anything regarding your financial obligations, any of your debts in this premarital agreement, did you?"

A. "Yes, there are statements." You could see he was preparing himself for the onslaught regarding this subject because of how he crossed his hands as resistance, not giving away his real intentions.

Q. "There were no attachments that dealt with what your debts were, what your financial obligations were - none of those attachments were there. We checked."

A. "Uh-huh."

Q. "There is nothing in the attachments to this alleged premarital agreement. There're no attachments related to the wife's assets, liabilities or income. No discloser, all the relevant information that you should attached to your documents, you attached after your wife moved out... the lineup of the pages proves it."

A. "I didn't know what the benefit of doing that was." He danced around the questions, steering himself out of the interrogation by not saying much. Other than boldly used 'anyway' to tamp down his answers and move on.

It was an internal need to find something else to shift the incriminating light of blame. He put on an act, like performing in the theater. His tone changed; he spoke with a condescending voice to demean me. Everything he had tried to conceal during the marriage was on full display. He was the one who violated my rights, yet on the stand, accusing me of the things that described him. He was making untrue statements, even when his depositions and voice on the tape opposed him.

Mr. Grant: "Play another part of the tape." Everyone

held onto their breath as the next part of the exchange was played. Once the relevant part was through, he paused the audio and resumed his cross-examination.

Q. "Did you hear yourself? Now you testified that she didn't have any problem with signing any document. This is your testimony... is that correct?"

A. "Correct, I gave her a photocopy as well as the original copy," he repeated to support his delusional views.

Deception had seeped deep into his soul and he couldn't be honest. We were pressing for narrow gleams of honesty, perhaps a bit of shame when clear-as-day evidence contradicted him, yet he remained shameless. When he was asked to explain his actions, he was annoyed and guarded himself by putting his hand over his mouth. His lawyer reminded him that we couldn't hear him, he took his hands off his mouth, found his mouth once again. He was told not to do it, but his body language was in the paranoid phase. He almost lost it on the stand when he was forced to answer the questions.

Mr. Duncan: "The document speaks for itself."

Judge: "I think they do, too. What is he going to add to

what he has already said?"

Mr. Grant: "Well, I think it shows the attitude about the agreement and I think it's relevant to the unconscionability, the circumstances surrounding the execution of the agreement, the sharp practices that we are going to prove through other evidence here."

Judge: "Objection sustained. It's my view that is the important one."

Q. "You were deposed at great length about the circumstances leading up to the preparation of this agreement. At no point did you ever say that you had prepared what you had brought back and discussed with her. At no point in your deposition did you tell us about that?"

Mr. Duncan: "I think if you are going to impeach him, you need to say if you were asked about it."

Mr. Grant: "I can go through a part of his deposition where I think it would be prompted by that."

Q. "Now, it's your testimony that you both had made changes in it? What changes did she have to make?"

A. "Well, for example she put in the statement about adultery by the husband."

Q. "Do you recall testifying earlier that it was your idea to put a revision in that adultery as it voided the agreement? Remember, it was your idea to put it in?"

Mr. Grant: "Your Honor, if I may... I want to find that question."

Q. "In your deposition, I asked you at the bottom of page 15, line 23, "And you met with this lawyer how many times prior to this agreement being prepared?" Your answer was, "We met probably three or four times. Every time it was different until, you know, for example, in that thing on adultery, it wasn't there. I added that one myself you know." Under oath, you testified that you insisted on that provision being in there, is that correct?"

A. "I insisted because... because I had no intention of committing adultery."

He became very edgy, and began throwing one of his classic tantrums. I was somewhat eager to see if Alan can control the situation with his huffing and puffing in the courtroom. His expressions got gloomy, and his voice became a series of whiny noises. This long face was the result of practice over many years' worth of manipulative behavior. There wasn't a line of dignity he wouldn't cross if he could gain sympathy from the judge. He jumbled so many irrelevant details that the judge asked him to be quiet; he still kept talking defensively.

Q. "You committed adultery with a woman named Melina, did you not?"

Mr. Duncan: "Your Honor, I must object to that."

Mr. Grant: "Your Honor, the agreement by its terms states that it's void if he's committed adultery. This question is relevant."

Judge: "The issue is whether the agreement is valid or not. Let's move on."

Mr. Grant: "If it's valid, we can litigate that later."

He knew the sleazy side of Alan; he didn't want him to gain credibility through the deceptive behavior. He wanted to make sure the judge saw the irony, and not give him a pass for falsifying evidence. Mostly to hear the bizarre answers Alan gave in his deposition when asked about adultery.

Q. "Did you have extra marital affair?"

A. "No, the issue never came up until you saw that statement in my prenuptial agreement."[5]

Q. "Who was that postcard from?"

A. "Oh, I wrote the postcard, it was from me to me, he laughed gracelessly. I asked somebody in the hospital write the letter for me to get attention from my wife."

Q. "So you manipulated your wife, you think it's okay to toy with someone's feeling if you gain by it."

A. "Well, works for me, he whispered."

Nothing was grounded in actual facts; he just made up stories to mask the truth. For every charge we made, he made nonsensical counter charges to make himself look good. Yet everything he said was at odds with the facts. His lawyer was aware of his client's dishonesty, but still had to defend him. In order to shield him, any time we tried to dispute Alan's claims with facts, he would have an

---

[5] He admitting that his wife never had the document to know about such clause, else she would make an added ground for divorce.

objection to distract the judge – as if he knew that the judge wouldn't examine the evidence. The sad part was that the judge often repeated the same thing, "*let the evidence speak for itself.*"

When I was on the stand, he used the court's time to promote his client as a decent doctor who cared for his wife. Then he went to great length to smear me, his round of inquiries was absurdly rude and bizarre. Once he got to questioning me about drinking, he actually got testy.

Q. "So whatever it was, you calmed down. How much wine have you ever had?"

A. "Well, I have a very low tolerance for alcohol, and Alan knows that. It's not a secret."

Q. "He didn't force you to drink. He offered you a glass of wine, and you said 'Sure?'"

A. "He didn't force me. He brought me a glass of wine and poured one for himself."

Q. "Is that what a glass of wine does to you?"

A. "It's enough alcohol to affect my functionality, possibly something was in the drink. How do I know with this document, he must have done something?"

Q. "Your testimony is that the last thing you remember about this episode is you were going somewhere?"

A. "Yes, that's all I remember."

Q. "But you do remember getting in the car, right? Then you went to Chicago, correct?"

A. "Day after."

Q. "Okay, so you understood him to tell you that you signed the premarital agreement?"

A. "No, he didn't mention it at all."

Q. "Okay, so let me ask you this - when you were riding to Chicago on the 22nd, and he mentioned you had signed something, what did you think you signed?"

A. "I assumed it was the document he had brought to me nine months prior, when I had gotten angry with him over it..."

Q. "Whatever that document was, you told him the day before to call off the wedding?"

A. "Yes, I did."

Q. "You are a college instructor. You read newspapers. You read books. You read enough back nine months before your marriage to know you were not going to agree with the terms of what was in that document. You understood that it was not fair and it was insulting."

A. "It was insulting, because he told me he doesn't have any money, and I didn't see the point to be disrespected for a lousy $50,000 he paid for a down-payment. Marriage is a partnership, we take risks and reap the rewards at the same time, together."

Q. "Did you understand that's the document that was presented to you, nine months before your marriage said? You understood that, didn't you?"

A. "I understood because the document he brought nine months before wasn't this one. I didn't approve that document, why would I want to agree with this one. It waives away my rights regardless of my medical and financial condition; even waive away my basic needs during the marriage. Sorry sir, this document is so grossly unfair that no-one would agree to it."

Q. "Okay, so the document nine months ago, you

waived those rights away as well, did you not?"

A. "That document was like a promissory note. I pay my student loan, and he keeps his down-payment on the house. There was nothing about what he has in this document. He just unilaterally waived all my rights in the marriage."

Q. "My question to you is, did you tell him on the 23rd that you weren't going to marry him?"

A. "I was wondering whether or not I had to marry this man. I didn't like the sneaky side of him."

Judge: "The question is. Did you say that to him?"

A. "No. I thought it was the document on the coffee table, the one allowed him to keep his $50,000 down-payment, and I pay my student loan."

Q. "Did you tell him you were not going through with the wedding?"

A. "As I said I was wondering about it; I didn't like his deceptive nature. At the last minute to pull a fast one. Unfortunately, it was too late. Our family and friends were in Chicago, he still did the unthinkable, and let me reiterate that the document on the table wasn't this one."

Q. "Let me ask you this question. You say he promised to give you the house after you got married?"

A. "Yes, he said as soon as we married, I will add your name to the house. Once we married, he said you have to change your last name, before adding your name to the house and financial documents. I changed my last name, and waited for him to fulfill his obligations. Then he said adding your name to the house cost $5,000, but fourteen years later I found out it was just $400."

Q. "Well, with regard to the Ph.D... did that induce you to marry him or to sign a document?"

A. "If I knew that he would disagree with my career advancements, I wouldn't have married him."

Q. "You are a pretty strong woman, are you not? Not easily intimidated, right?"

A. "I am a strong woman, that's why he hid his agenda."

Q. "So you were intending on marrying a sugar daddy then, weren't you? You were marrying him for his money, is that correct? That is what you wanted, isn't it?"

A. "I did all the work. Sugar daddies take care of their

wives, but he put all of the obligations on my shoulders, while behind my back, he abdicated all his responsibilities to me. What kind of husband would do that?"

Q. "Your position remains that he deceived you... he lied to you? He got you drunk and drugged you?"

A. "That's exactly it. I didn't know if some sort of sleep-inducing drug was in the drink."

As the questioning went on, he kept making snarky comments to play hardball.

Q. "Did you pay rent while you were married?" he asked in a cartoonish way.

When I tried to respond, he demanded a simple "yes" or "no" answer, as if I was some kind of logic machine. I was trying to explain the situation, but he kept on interrupting me until I finished my words to his liking. I felt bullied by his ranting and belligerent tactics. Obviously, he didn't want the judge to hear me so tried to rush me through the answers to misinform the judge.

A. "I did all the work. Alan trapped me into his game without my consent, and then closed the door to establish his entitlement to our financial assets, and in the process making me weak. No decent human being bases their life's plan on the failure of someone else."

Q. "You are a strong headed woman, are you not?"

This question almost sounded like an attack to portray me in a negative light. He was trying to make me crack by echoing the same nonsense Alan had told him, and I was doing my utmost to not allow that to happen.

A. "My husband was a nightmare during the marriage," I expressed my emotions of frustration.

Suddenly, he accused me of something it wasn't true, and I wanted to defend myself from his charges, but something in me didn't want to argue. I realized he was doing his job, protecting a con man. As soon as I finished, he put Alan on the stand.

Q. "Is it true you were a nightmarish husband?"

A. "I was the best husband," he answered smugly.

His voice on the transcript is barely audible. Any normal person may have humbly said, I did the best I could, but he had to promote himself as the best. He bypassed the drunkenness and his deceitful conduct during the marriage, and jumping directly into self-promotion. Listening to his testimony to mock the court was unsettling, it reminded me of how he had deceived me.

An expert forensic document examiner, Mr. Hudson was called on the stand to testify on my behalf. He said, "I examined the signature on the alleged Premarital Agreements (Defendant's Exhibits 1 and 2), and compared the signatures to known handwriting samples. My examination and analysis indicated that whoever wrote the signatures was using what is referred to as a stroke impulse to write some of the letters, and they were not comfortable or did not know how to write certain letters in a normal and natural way as the writer of the known writings did. Additionally, the two questioned signatures on Defendant's Exhibits 1 and 2 appear to be simulations."

The other side had their own forensic document examiner. He was called to the stand and asked whether the signatures on the defendant's Exhibit 1 and 2 were made by the person who signed the known documents. In his own words, "My conclusion was, due to unexplained variations, I wasn't able to determine that…"

Alan's agenda to turn my own friends, my own daughter,

and even his children against me, didn't work. But his idea worked with Sherry and her husband. I have no doubt he played them like a fiddle, portraying himself as a victim to draw them in. To use them and his sister as a cheerleader, to do his bidding. These are the same people who were deeply involved in his previous marriage. It's ironic, how everything comes back to the same cast of characters played before. Savile was the one always cleaning after him, and her testimony was full of crap, no surprises there. She was the beneficiary of half of our marital assets, the least she could do was to recycle her brother garbage and cover-up for him.

Even the testimony of Verne, Sherry's husband, was okay. I respected him for defending his friend and telling the truth, but I can't say the same about Sherry. What she did was rude, no real friend would go beyond that boundary in friendship to dish out utter lies. An honest friend would do the opposite. Evidently, she was rooting for my failure, so interjected herself into my life to pass judgment and make herself relevant.

It's easier to focus on someone else's problem than look at her own life and correct herself. I remember when she told me, "*I didn't marry my husband because I loved him. I just wanted a better life, and he was my getaway car.*" Her advice to me, "*pretend you are okay.*" Obviously, pretending works very well for her - living behind her layers of facades regardless of what's in her heart. As an alternative, she surrounded herself with material life to forget about her emotional fakeness. I don't have that much talent for posing artificially as it is something that instinctively repulses me.

Outside the courtroom, Sherry told Sara, "*I did ask Alan for a copy of whatever he had, but he refused. I know he lied.*" Then inside the court when Mr. Grant asked her that question, she contradicted herself over the matter, "*I never asked, it wasn't my place to ask.*" She showed no awareness of her doing, other than indulging herself in dishonesty. This stemmed from something deeper, it was her bitterness that had drawn her to court, in order to express her sense of resentment for disrupting her social circle. "*You are ruining my social life,*" she told me before my move out. I don't think she knew how annoying she was - my move out was not about her.

Clearly, her fixations got in the way of telling the truth.

"*Your mother is my best friend*," she felt the need to tell Sara. Who needs friends like that? My life is challenging enough that I don't have to deal with so-called friend. I prefer an honest enemy over a phony friend. Her emotional coldness is her coping mechanism. In her deposition she downplayed my career aspiration in order to alleviate herself. She didn't have enough decency to ask me before passing sweeping judgments.

It was a teachable moment for me, when Sherry showed up in court to testify against me. I realized that women can be as sexist as men are - more forgiving of men's wrongdoing as long as they aren't their own husband. She went to the gutter to undermine me just to impress those who had rejected her for years. Desperately wanting to be accepted among those that had insulted her, she wound up expressing the same thing, hoping by bashing me she will gain membership to their special club. I truly regret the time I had wasted on her.

It looked like what Alan was carrying in himself was contagious among this bunch of friends. They have the same symptoms and share the same mannerisms as they all are cut from the same cloth - neon. Flashy, it's all about the appearances - to be more by having more. They surrounded themselves with their possessions, yet lacked social skills. Their opinions of others were based on whether they were the haves or the have-nots. Trapped into their status-based thinking – the other person must be a doctor, married to a doctor, or both. They made sure others called them 'doctor,' too, which proves their sense of insecurity. They always noticed who didn't call them by their self-imposed rank. Probably saw themselves in others, that blinded them to the reality, not everyone is like them.

The judge allowed both sides to submit written arguments in support of their respective positions. Before making his ruling on the authenticity of the signatures. I told the judge that I never entered into such a contract to waive my rights. To help the judge to understand the anti-wife plots, I offered to take polygraph tests to prove I had been conned.

A month later, the Judge send us his ruling: "*The plaintiff's burden of proving her case by "clear and convincing evidence. In summary, she has carried her burden of establishing by clear and convincing evidence that the alleged Agreement is unenforceable under Va.*

Code Ann. 20-151 (1950, as Amended). Both parties called handwriting experts who had examined Wife's purported signature on the Agreement. Neither expert could positively confirm nor exclude Wife as being the writer of the signatures on the Agreement..."

"Wife urges generally that she did not sign the Agreement, and additionally argues several alternative theories for non-enforcement: (1) the Agreement is unconscionable; (2) the Husband's fraud and duress; (3) abandonment or repudiation; and (4) void ability on account of Husband's adultery. In response, Husband contends that Wife executed the Agreement with a full and clear understanding of its terms, particularly the financial consequences upon divorce. In Virginia "courts will not invalidate a premarital contract because subsequent history discloses that the contractual provisions are 'ill-reasoned or ill-advised." The Court is satisfied that Wife actually signed the Agreement in her right mind and was given an opportunity, whether she took it or not, to review its terms before she signed it."

His decision caught me entirely by surprise, I expected that justice would be on my side. In the courtroom, the judge gave the impression of being a serious man, even though I saw him give more leeway to the other side. They often objected to our arguments to suppress the evidence. In many instances when we tried to bring the judge's attention to the truth, and the judge was in a position to ask for clarification, he instead echoed the objection of the other side and impatiently asking us to 'move on.' Still, I never predicted such an illogical decision, and surely didn't expect accusations without merit.

I thought judges have the responsibility to investigate motives. I was the injured party, the one ushered into falsehood during the marriage. My legal dispute demanded care from the judge. To see my husband's fraudulent behavior in taking advantage of the loopholes in Virginia's laws, and his voice on the tape verified his deceptions. The judge had witnessed all the lies and contradictions from defendant as he perjured himself on the stand, yet he ruled as if he had not been there in the courtroom.

I wondered, what the judge's motive had been in siding with the defendant. During the court's proceeding we stuck to the facts, and the other side denied them. I was hoping the judge wouldn't buy into Alan's gamesmanship, but obviously he bought the image wholeheartedly. Their tricks of false statements and denials worked, they sold a fake document as authentic. We provided ample proof of Alan's misdeeds yet the judge, instead of sifting through the evidence to look for accuracy, he accused me of 'giving away my rights,' when all the evidence proved otherwise.

The court system is supposed to protect people from injustice, not be a tool of prejudice. My voice was ignored, my rights were taken away, and my judgment has been compromised – so much so that I've had to question myself. The judge was the one who had no moral courage to see the crime, because if he looked at the clues we provided, he wouldn't have judged against me.

Despite my best efforts to stay calm, going back to the court stressed me out. I had no idea how abusive divorce courts could be. The emotional impact of insults in each court proceeding drained all my energy. The only thing left to argue in the court was centered on the unconscionability of fraudulent documents, and the breach of his own contract. The adultery was the rule Alan set to void his phony contract. He had confessed in his deposition that I never had the document, until I filed for the divorce. The judge didn't allow us to question him on that subject, but I was hoping he would read the transcripts and reconsider his decision.

On the last day of the court, the judge said, *"No more evidence."* Then, halfway through the final court hearing, Alan threw an accusation that he provided me with four credit cards, and he paid for all those bills. It was a lie. I felt the flash of fury on my face certainly, I didn't want him to have another victory at my expense.

Mr. Grant: *"Do you have any proof."*

Alan: *"I'm telling you my wife used those cards."*

Mr. Grant: *"If those are her cards, let me see."*

Alan refused to hand over the cards, until his lawyer told him, *"If her name is on them, she should have them."*

I couldn't believe the level of egotism that we should trust him because he said so. To defend myself against his lies, during the break I called the credit card company, to find out how he had gotten those cards. I was told: *"the cards never been used by an authorized name, and some cards are from fourteen years back."*

I returned to the courtroom to tell Mr. Grant about the trick Alan had pulled, that he was secretly collecting evidence to have a defense for the future, prove to the judge that he'd been a caring husband. Surely, in his mind, he's a man of many talents.

I was so offended by what Alan did, yet many of the questions couldn't be asked outright in the courtroom. When the court was in recess, I expressed my annoyance: *"What you did is another one of your deceitful acts. You think everybody in the court is stupid. When did you learn this technique of conning, that you become so expert?"* As soon as the court reconvened, they withdraw their claim.

Life goes on with a blend of good and evil. I was thrilled when I heard I will be a grandmother soon. My enthusiasm about her birth excited me, and cheerfully counted the days until her birth. The day Kara born was one of the most touching moments of my life. The second I saw that sweet baby, I felt I had gained a treasure, and once again my world became a beautiful place. I realized that regardless of our ups and downs in life, we should never lose sight of what's important. I hoped that my troubles would soon be over so that I would have time for the things that really matter.

Two months later, I got a call from my brother that my mother had passed away. I felt terrible for not having an opportunity to say goodbye in person. I was planning to go for a visit, a chance to see her and comfort her, but it was too late. My mother was sick for almost six months. I talked to her every day, and then when she got very ill, I talked to her whenever she was conscious. The agony of her sickness made her helpless. I remember my mother when she was so strong and a symbol of grace. Then at the peak of her wisdom her body began to fail, she suffered so much that she desired to die, but it was not her time. My sisters watched her battle against death; she wasn't scared, just ready to go and she died peacefully.

I got there the night before her funeral, the sadness of not seeing her for the last time was heavy on me. Out of exhaustion from the long trip I passed out. I felt my mother's presence in the room, sitting there in silence and looking at me. I recognized her kind face. She calmly whispered, *"Our guests are waiting."* There was a sudden surge of love in my heart, and then she was gone. When I woke up, the overriding emotion of spending time with my mother made me calm down.

I felt she knew I was there for her funeral, and her visit had a mystical meaning - not to feel guilty for my absence during her last days here on earth. Having that dream the night before her funeral gave me the feeling that she was there with me in spirit, and made the next day easier for me. I thought that maybe my mother was in a better place and this is what she wanted, but I was still filled with a sense of regret about not spending enough time with her.

It's nice to be someone's child, never too old to need them. I always listened to her attentively to absorb her insight. When she was alive and well, I didn't want to take anything for granted. So, whenever I found an opportunity, I asked her to repeat those words of wisdom to write them down. For me, those are the best gifts. Many of her advice is carved into my brain, and sometimes in the middle of the night I hear my mother in her quiet voice.

Chapter 11
Final Judgment From Court

After many months of waiting for the court's final verdict, the judge confirmed our worst fears by ruling that we didn't prove our case beyond a reasonable doubt. His verdict drained hope out of me. The burden of proof was on my shoulders, we put so much effort to get the truth, yet it didn't have any effect on his decision. He was blinded by his own preconceptions, and no amount of information was enough to judge fairly.

He simply painted both sides in the marriage with the same brush, and find equal fault. "*Both deserve an equal share of the blame*," the judge said to disguise his biased emotions. Then he took the positions of, "*I don't know what to believe*," to set the tone of his preference to accept the husband's argument. It conveniently fit into the narrative of what he wanted to believe. He selectively chose items from the defendant's argument to justify his erroneous ruling. It was his way of dispensing with a complicated case, an easy out at my expense.

Judges are supposed to have moral authority, and not give a wrongdoer a free pass. Yet, there is no legal pressure to be evenhanded in their decisions; they can use their power to make any judgment they desire. Throughout the trial, I thought that the judge was listening and advocating for truth. But his final verdict reveal that his mind made up way before finalizing the case. It seemed he prejudged the case once he took side with the defendant, and afterward, nothing changed his mind. He still sat there as a symbolic gesture that he respected the process of hearing both sides, when he already had the conclusion. So, his moral posturing during the court hearing was insincere, and we were wasting energy on a battle that was already lost.

He used his position as a judge to exercise ultimate power. He sidestepped the evidence, including the testimony of the two forensic examiners, which they explained in details that the signature on the alleged document can't be proven as being mine. Our document examiner illustrated with many screenshots, that the dubious signature on the alleged document is a simulation. The judge, instead of looking for truth and weighing the opinions of the two experts, casually dismissed their testimony to confirm his own opinion, which was grounded in false assumptions. His rigid mindset prevented him from seeing the truth, even though the facts were right in front of his eyes, it was his choice to ignore the it.

He failed to recognize that the state of Virginia doesn't have the safety and requirements of other states. Virginia's laws have so many loopholes that anyone with a criminal mind can easily take advantage of. In fact, at the time, state didn't require those contract signatures to be on the same page or even the same day. Many states require a notary page with a brief description of the document, the name of a lawyer on the documents, and the initial of the signatories on every page. Virginia does not. Some states require a record of the notary log, or a copy of documents to be stored in the courthouse or lawyer office. But Virginia doesn't require any of those things, which makes forgery very easy[6].

---

[6] In 2008 law amended, closed the loophole for the notaries. Now all signature should be in the same page.

A Sample of the Judge's Statements:

"Throughout the marriage, Wife seemed concerned about her financial security. Wife looked into the possibility of obtaining a Ph.D. in the hope of gaining greater earning potential as a teacher. She discovered that that their household income precluded her from obtaining scholarships to further her education on her own. When she broached the idea to Husband, he vetoed it, claiming that Wife needed to be at home for him..."

"Wife urges that Husband should be stopped from seeking to enforce the premarital agreement due to his conduct...Somethings are clear. Husband jealously guarded the privacy of his financial situation and kept the state of his separate accounts hidden from Wife. Wife was obligated to run the household, provide for the landscaping and improvements to the home, and entertain guests..."

"Wife urges here that Husband's statements that he would give her a copy of the agreement, that he had "torn up" the agreement, The Court is persuaded that Husband said these things to Wife" but "Wife is chargeable with the knowledge of what the law requires for an effective revocation. Code Section 20-153 provides that."

First, the judge signaled that it is okay for women to be oppressed, "...*husband did not like the career of the wife, and wanted attention.*" The judge not seeing anything wrong with such demand, because he rewarded him instead of punishing him. He undermined wife's ambition for career progress as if the wife is the problem, implying that the husband is entitled to her flexibility and he should have the advantage where he sees fits.

Then, when it comes to the husband's deceitful acts, the judge was unable to acknowledge his oppressive behavior, and looked for excuses to defend his faulty judgment. "*The wife is chargeable with the knowledge of what the law requires,*" he said. Suddenly, the wife was equally in charge when the evidence proved otherwise. The judge never asked himself how the wife would survive, if she gave up both her career objectives and her marital rights to financial security.

Like any other profession judges can be arrogant too, and we can't count on their sincerity. The voice of a person to confess to his wrongdoing is a powerful piece of evidence, yet the judge ignored it. His approach to the case was more about man versus woman, rather than wrong versus right. Apparently in civil court, there is no penalty for being an outright liar. That makes it easy for a judge to deliver a fact-free ruling. In his courtroom, the mockery of the legal system was allowed, lying under oath didn't matter. Perjury didn't count as a serious offense. The contradictions in the testimony didn't trouble the judge, despite the evidence we presented. He was unwilling to accept any evidence that might contradict his preconceived ideas about the case.

What makes a judge side with the person who defied the law? In my case, the ideology about a woman's secondary place in society aligned him with the defendant, the person who had deceived me. The lens he used right from the start was based on his personal theories. He assumed that the defendant did nothing wrong, so instead of investigating the issues he accepted his words, and truth lost its place under his disregard. The judge never put himself in my shoes to see the evidence from my side. He blamed the woman in justifying his judgment, *"as ill as this document is, wife signed it,"* he said. According to him, it is the wife's fault that the husband claims everything, 'she has given away her rights.' His dogma blinded him to admit that some men are bound to be con artists.

In the court system, bigotry is still a lingering infection among judges, and many courtroom fights demonstrate this bias in their rulings. Perhaps injustice is a more common practice in the south than other places. When we don't have enough female judges to be sympathetic to women's causes, and men are still controlling the courts. So anytime we are faced with legal issues, we become the target of their critical remark. Here I was, conned during my marriage, stripped of my rights, and I still have to take this nonsense from a judge, who clearly had an obsolete world view in treating one gender with such contempt, while favoring the other gender.

His double standards made a fair trial impossible. Instead of coming to grips with the reality that there are fundamental problems with Virginia laws, he turned into an echo chamber for the lawbreaker, and ignored the truth that the defendant manipulated the laws. I saw a minister of justice in action, accepting falsehoods of a pathological liar as gospel truth, while striking down my fact-based claims. To whitewash his prejudice, he lectured me about the rule of law, *"Job of the court is not about protecting people from their own decision...*" His righteous posturing as an angel of justice was his way to hold me liable, to suggest that I brought this on myself.

My case is proof that this judge gave the benefit of the doubt to the husband. No matter how much evidence I had on my side, never enough to defend me. He showed more sympathy for the person who made a fraudulent document, than the person harm by such a document. Losing my rights to a con artist, who claimed everything was separate property, and then seeing the judge take his side was like rubbing salt into my wound. One doesn't easily recover from this kind of ruthless treatment. People were telling me maybe the judge was paid off, to have issued such an extreme ruling. I will never know if that was the case, so I have to make my peace with it.

What I do know is, a reasonable judge wouldn't ignore my contributions to the marriage, and before throwing out our arguments, would look at the totality of what happened in the case. A fair-minded judge would have considered all the relevant facts, the tape, depositions, financial records, and circumstance surrounding the way the alleged document was produced. Our judge didn't use the same moral rules that other judges apply in their courtroom; he ignored the evidence in order to reinforce his point of view. In his ruling he cited: *"Wife was allowed to use credit cards in her own name and bore responsibility for paying these debts. She was from time to time unable to perform her duties on the monies provided by her husband and her own funds, and she ran up significant balances on her charge and credit card accounts."* Then, he dismissed my claim to count the debts during the marriage as marital.

He used his platform as a personal quest to deny me the rights. His failure on investigating the evidence proved that his emotion of gender bias was stronger than being judicious. He put his stamp of approval on the wrongdoer of his gender, yet not enough respect for a woman to be objective. My right in the marriage was confiscated based on a fake document. No one should have to put up with such abuse. It is reasonable that a judge count on people to do the right thing, but it isn't reasonable when a judge takes man's words as truth regardless of facts against him. That's inexcusable.

His hostile verdict intended to suppress my voice in the marriage, and to blame me was his way of easing his guilty conscience. To fight back against his ruling, we hired an extra lawyer to help us with the appeal. I was hoping judges in the appellate court would see things differently. I wanted to prove to myself that the real justice exists, and one unfair judge doesn't mean all judges are unfair.

However, the judge constrained our case for the appeal. He framed his decision in such a way that we couldn't challenge his first verdict on the signature. The man of law used the rule of law to defend his unfair decision – it shows the level of control the lower courts have. Two capable lawyers couldn't convince the judge to be fair; he instead limited us in legal proceedings. But we still continued with the appeal.

Proposed grounds for appeal
- Conflicting decisions by judge.
- Ignoring the evidence.
- Misapplication of the law.
- Conflicting statements by defendants' witnesses.
- Material change in conditions of agreement.
- Agreement was not signed consciously and voluntarily.

A sample of the argument for appeal: *"Judge narrowed questioning and refused to hear matters in which he ultimately rendered a decision...why he chose to believe the defendant, who was impeached multiple times on the witness stand and on tape, over the statements and evidence presented by wife. It's peculiar that the judge would admit the audio tape and expert reports only to completely ignore it in his decision..."*

Despite the restrictions inhibiting our appeal, we still hoped the 'Court of Appeals' would deliver a different outcome. Obviously, it was too much to ask when they didn't have all the relevant facts. It's tough to have an impartial hearing in the court of a small town. Once someone get away with misconduct, it's hard to prove beyond a reasonable doubt with an unreasonable judge, who lacked the talent to see an obvious crime.

I believe Alan got the idea of defrauding me from a story that I once told him before marrying him. The story was about one of my father's clients. She was informed by friends that her husband had a second wife. A second marriage was illegal, except in the case of the first wife's infertility or with the permission of the first wife. In this case, the wife already had four children from her husband and she had not given permission to marry a second wife.

When my father took the case to court, her husband brought a piece of paper with his wife's fingerprint. He announced it was his wife that allowed him to have a second wife. She was puzzled about how her husband had gotten her fingerprint, since she would never agree to something like that. Then she remembered a year before, one morning, when she woke up her finger had an ink mark on it. With four kids at home, she thought she got the ink mark from one of the kids' projects. It became clear to her that was her husband's trickery. When she was sleep, he fingerprinted the document, and married a second wife without her consent.

Alan copied that idea, and put a lot of time into his horrid plan. In his delusional world marriage was a war zone, and his wife was the enemy. He armed himself with a bogus document, and used it as a weapon in the grand battle of marriage to avoid accountability. A preemptive strike to get the desired outcome. To push his agendas, used the misleading tactics to deprive me from informed decisions, so that he could covertly take away all the risk from himself, and hang on my neck by misinforming. He practiced the techniques of detachment, which the army uses in wars to train soldiers not to empathize with the enemy. Alan used the same methodology, to maximize his benefits and have the advantage over his marriage.

The facade he presented on the surface was a calculated plan to delay my reaction to his doings. He believed there is no cost to him if his scheme were hidden from me. I recall a few years back he said something very relevant, but at the time his words didn't resonate with me. He told me about a woman who used to work with him at the hospital, and she had extramarital affairs. *"Aren't you afraid what would happen if your husband found out?"* Alan had asked. *"What my husband doesn't know won't hurt him or me,"* she answered. Judging from his falsified document, this was his method of deceit, too.

If the court system worked, Alan wouldn't have a free pass for being a good actor and a big schemer. The ethical bars are so low that anyone can game the system. These kinds of judges are the reason for a dysfunctional court system which feeds the fantasies of con artists. Alan came to court to manipulate the judge the same way he did with his marriage. In that aspect, he succeeded, outfoxing the judge with his dazzling performance. The morally bankrupt liar prospered far beyond his wildest dreams. Nothing was more significant to him than being validated by a judge and collecting his prizes for being a conman.

I could never have predicted that the court system would be so flawed. Judges were supposed to be smarter than those of us going to them for advice. Yet, he was duped by the same person who duped me, and I have to pay for the judge's ignorance. It's a sad reality that people get away with their crime. I wish I had pursued a criminal lawsuit, instead of a civil one.

Finally, after many twists and turns, my divorce with Alan was finalized. Still, he was sending notes to aggravate me and make himself relevant. To have a sense of closure I responded back, to make it clear that my life no longer is about his pitiful mind games.

Chapter 12
Where I Go From Here

I have to adjust to injustice. I cannot undo the damage, but I have to look at the world from a different angle, and recognize the complexity of human nature far beyond my own naive lens. It's hard to admit that people we trust could treat us so unkindly. Thus, we have to be more cautious about who we invite into our life, at a time when decency is a rare commodity.

Regrettably the lack of sympathy for others has spread like a virus, and this has even reached judges in the courtroom. I have never been more discouraged about the court system than I am at this point in my life. The system is so broken that there's no objectivity. It's no wonder that people have given up on the legal system and take matters into their own hands. They have nowhere to go. I sympathize with them as I myself suffered from a lapse of justice, and lost confidence in the integrity of the justice system.

It's a reminder that the progress for women isn't deep

enough to feel safe, and what happened to me could happen to anyone. Equality doesn't mean anything when we are overruled by judges whose rulings lack justice. The culture is shifting, but still, many judges cling to their power to keep up with the false narrative of the role of woman in society. It is a travesty that many of us are working and also have a big responsibility at home, yet when it comes to financial security, our voices aren't valued. Judges take sides in gender conflicts, to undermine our efforts in the marriage and society as a whole.

Judges are supposed to be the defenders of society, not the oppressors. If we cannot find impartiality and fair treatment in the courts, then where can we find it? When the only remedy we have fails us. We should speak out; otherwise, our silence validates their actions and keeps them in power. Then our suffering never ends and keeps coming back to haunt us. We ought to work harder and leave a legacy of a fairer society than what we found.

The judge's verdict triggered outrage in me and emboldened me to express my worries regarding the abuse of power. I saw it as a duty to speak out against those who denied me the truth. Writing a book is my way of getting justice and letting my voice be heard. It's my intention to shine a light on judicial bias in the court system. We all desire that wrongdoers to be punished, but due process is absent from many courtrooms. They act righteously as men of law, but their own agenda dictates their ruling. Easily let the guilty go free while innocents pay the price.

I'm embarrassed with what I witnessed. The culture of exclusion isn't something any of us want in the social fabric. We have to stand up to mean spirited judges, and publicly declare that what they are doing isn't acceptable. We deserve judges with the courage to be a voice for human dignity and advocate for social changes. Perhaps more women should be on the bench of power, to replace the radical judges and balance out the male-dominated atmosphere. I've no doubt seen female judges put more effort into their work, to survive amidst man's supremacy.

What took place in my life brought me so many life-changing lessons. A chance to tell my story through the lens of experience. I'm a teacher at heart, and life has put me in a different path to instill something in me. What did I learn from my experience that I can convey to others? My story is a cautionary tale, and I hope it encourages you to seek guidance on decisions affected by an arbitrary court system.

My Biggest Takeaways:

– Watch your back in the relationship, and don't let your guard down. Things may not work out exactly as you hope. It's hard to see a real person through their charming manners, so protect yourself with critical eyes as there might be no recovery from a downfall. I was unlucky, getting into the same pathway with the wrong person. Like many, I had a blind spot. My husband talked of a good life for us, and good just covered him. It's a different mindset when a person enters into a relationship with hostility, rather than love and trust.

– Don't ignore your gut feeling in any relationship. We all have a mystical element in us – a private eye within. Our body warns us about surrounding problems, and we should be cognizant of these physical symptoms. Love is safe and should be a peaceful place to be in, but it wasn't the way I felt. I recall many nights when my husband came to bed, I couldn't stay in bed. Part of it was his drinking but more was involved.

— Don't let a situation that someone else creates for you, define you. Our life is a gift to us, we should cherish our path and enjoy it as every day comes. Most people don't change, and we shouldn't change ourselves to accommodate them. Be cautious of the impulse to cave-in, in order to have a happy place in your life. Those who love you actually let you grow. I learned we cannot make someone else happy by giving up on our own ambition.

— For those of you, who see the half glass full in life, be wary. Don't rely on others; some people don't have the courage to do right by you. My experience has opened my eyes to human nature. We really don't know others, someone looking good from outside could be a rotten character inside. Be aware of the emotional disconnect in some people as they find joy in the misery of others. Weed out the toxic people in your life, to have room for those worthy of being there – those who love you.

– When it comes to friendship, be careful who you call friend. We believe our friends are concerned about us and would never hurt us. My experiences proved that to be wrong. We ought to watch out who we share our thoughts, and separate our solid friends from those who call themselves friends. A real friend enriches your life and standby you in time of need, not only when it's convenient. Just remember, it is the double-faced people who smile at you while wishing you harm. Lastly, be aware of those undermining you; it's their way to shift the focus away from their own failure.

I have been victimized, but I refuse to be a victim. What happened didn't diminish me; it just awakened me to the truth about myself. I accepted responsibility for my mistakes, and reclaimed control by getting rid of the barrier within, to live a life with a sense of fulfillment. My mother left me with an acute sense of awareness, *"There is a wisdom in everything happen to us."* I feel anything unfolding in my life is meant to teach me something when I had no courage to make the change. My financial setback is the price I paid to sober up.

Life has thrown a lot of punches at me, but I bounced back. I gained awareness through the depths of my hurdles to see things I couldn't see before. Out of my suffering comes the power of within, finding enough nerve to get rid of a fraudulent marriage. It was a gratifying moment as I walked away from that negative energy. I promised myself to not ever tolerate the bad behavior of others at my own expense. There is more to life than being a performer in someone else's world. We should never abandon inspiration, in pursuit of a peaceful life, there is no peace once we lose who we are.

Surely, I have lost a lot, but I gained a harmonious life. My quiet apartment became a sacred place to sleep well. It brings calmness into my daily routines. I have the freedom to make my own decisions to find harmony and peace in myself. Fortunately, I have many loyal friends, and I am grateful for their steadfast friendship over the years. I learned through my troubling time when I needed friends. My true friends showed up to cheer me up, and the rest disappeared as things crumbled.

Still optimistic about life, I enjoy it for what it is, not for what it's supposed to be. To have a sense of balance, I found outlets that diverted my attention to something more pleasant. I have a great appreciation for the outdoors; I go for a daily walk to be energized. My favorite time of the year is spring. I drive near the river, where there're plenty of butterflies and wildflowers. It is a feast for the eyes, the glory of nature draws me in and encourages me listen to the whispers. I find the mystical elements in nature. The way water moves forward against the obstacles, it stirs me to let go of painful experiences. The strength of mountains and the harmony among them, emboldens me to stay strong and be open to possibilities.

The tranquility and wonders of nature always comfort my heart, and I never get tired of the natural surroundings. In Virginia, most of the trees change color in fall. They sparkle with different shades of colors that are extraordinarily beautiful − as if somebody had painted them. Who wouldn't love such a dazzling display? It certainly raises my spirits; it's a clue that with all the ugliness in the world, we can still find plenty of beauty to enjoy.

On a happier note, once we have done with the hustle and bustle of the court case, Sara married someone she loved, Brayan. At first, we were looking for a wedding dress to have a big event. I got excited about the process, and Sara enjoyed it, too. As we got closer to the details, she changed her mind, insisted on not letting me pay for it and go overboard with the spending – as most parents do. She settled on a destination wedding, still wearing an ivory beach gown.

When they returned, we celebrated their wedding in a small gathering. Sara wore a long white dress, just the way I always imagined her. It was a beautiful sight to behold, and many pictures captured the memory of that day. Now, they have a sweet little girl, Hana. Shan and his wife also have their second child – a sweet little boy, Arvin. Both babies were born in the same week; it was a double dosage of excitement for all of us.

These days, my injury isn't noticeable to most people. Against all the odds, I recaptured some of my lost life, enough to move on. I still have moments of anguish in which I feel I deserve better. Yet I don't let negativity seep into my psyche and keep me down. Perhaps it's the wisdom of age, that life is too short to let fears dictate my decisions. The insurance settlement wasn't nearly enough to pay for my legal fees, so I started teaching two classes to cover some of my bills. There have been many years of challenges, and I eventually learned to deal with it, by not pushing myself to the heights of exhaustion.

After my divorce, I was left with $78,000 in debt. However, I've something that money can't buy, the warmth of my family and the abundance of sincere friends. The most gratifying time of my life is when I'm with my family, they're in my thoughts in every waking moment. On top of it, I have the honor of three precious grandchildren that I adore. I never imagined I could enjoy anybody after my children, although the birth of each one added more delight to my heart.

It's a gift to be a grandparent. In their presence my problem disappears, and I integrated into their world as if I were a kid again — what a beautiful world it is. I take great pleasure in everything they do, overjoyed when I hear their laughter and running around. Impressed by their cuteness, and nothing could distract me from all the goodness I have with them. I feel the center of energy in my life is changing, and that gives me more reasons to smile.

WHERE I GO FROM HERE

www.ingramcontent.com/pod-product-compliance
Lightning Source LLC
LaVergne TN
LVHW041213080426
835508LV00011B/945